JOURNAL FOR THE STUDY OF THE OLD TESTAMENT
SUPPLEMENT SERIES

39

Editors
David J A Clines
Philip R Davies

Department of Biblical Studies
The University of Sheffield
Sheffield S10 2TN
England

THE SENSE OF BIBLICAL NARRATIVE:

Structural Analyses in the Hebrew Bible

David Jobling

Journal for the Study of the Old Testament
Supplement Series 39

Published by
JSOT Press
Department of Biblical Studies
The University of Sheffield
Sheffield S10 2TN
England

Typeset by JSOT Press
and
Printed in Great Britain
by Redwood Burn Ltd
Trowbridge, Wiltshire

British Library Cataloguing in Publication Data

Jobling, David
    The sense of the biblical narrative :
    structural analyses in the Hebrew Bible.
    —(Journal for the study of the Old Testament
    supplement series, ISSN 0309-0787; 39)
    2
    1. Bible. O.T.—Commentaries
    I. Title   II. Series
    221.6   BS1171.2

ISBN 1-85075-010-6
ISBN 1-85075-011-4 Pbk

To the staff of the Department of Biblical Studies
in the University of Sheffield
this book is affectionately dedicated

CONTENTS

INTRODUCTION

By these limited and partial analyses, we have hoped to suggest a certain manner of reading, a *methodological model* which seems to us, at present, the best adapted to the strategy of semiotic research: it consists, whenever one is confronted by a phenomenon which has not been analyzed, of constructing a representation of it in such a way that the model is more general than the case under examination requires, so that the observed phenomenon registers itself (*s'y inscrive*) as one of (the model's) variables (Greimas, 1976: 263).

1.   This book is a sequel to *The Sense of Biblical Narrative* (Jobling, 1978), which, having been for some time out of print, is now reappearing (as 'Volume I'). Like Volume I, Volume II contains three studies of separate origin, linked rather by commonality of method than of theme (though there is a narrow overlap between Chapters 2 and 3). Chapter 1 was born as a contribution to a symposium on Genesis 2–3 in the Structural Exegesis Seminar of the Society of Biblical Literature (Jobling, 1980b). A biblical text of such importance resists being simply the object of a methodological exercise, and I have expanded and recast the present version in the hope of its being a contribution to wider debate, particularly over feminist hermeneutics (§4). Chapter 2, which is new, treats the centrally important issue of Israel's political theory; it continues the line of research begun by 'Jonathan' (Vol. I/1). Chapter 3, prepared originally for the Centennial of the Society of Biblical Literature (Jobling, 1980a), is more obscure and difficult; obscure in theme and in the main texts it interprets, difficult in its variety of methods and its ultimate open-endedness. It was intended, as I explain in the introduction to the chapter, as a contribution to current debate over Israel's origins, albeit an oblique contribution, because of vast methodological problems. Whatever its success in this regard, I see it as the most ground-breaking of the three studies.

2.   How does Volume II represent an advance on Volume I? The question should be prefaced by the observation that Volume I is itself a different book in 1986 from 1978. What then appeared *avant garde* and difficult to many belongs now, I imagine, securely within a trend with which they have become familiar and even comfortable. In this sense, the new studies should be more accessible to readers in 1986 than the old ones were in 1978, for there is more continuity than discontinuity between the two volumes. The new ones are still not far from the mainstream of biblical structuralism, a stream which has been fed primarily from two sources: A.J. Greimas's literary analyses of the structures of narrativity, and Claude Lévi-Strauss's work on the semantic structure of myth. There are many now who regard this mainstream as conservative and outdated. During the rather long time that the book has been moving towards publication, my own methodological point of view has shifted enough to preclude my doing any more studies based on the same presuppositions as these. I put them forward for three reasons. First, for whatever exegetical value they may have. I have hoped to make exegetical gains in the reading of specific parts of the Bible—a consideration ignored by some methodophiles, but important to me. Second, much of the reaction against mainstream biblical structuralism has been based on falsely narrow conceptions of it, and I believe that it retains plenty of vigour provided it comes to terms with new methodological questions. Thirdly, these new studies adumbrate (and it is in this that they go beyond Volume I) the methodological shifts that are 'in the air'—much more than I realized as I wrote them. For the first of these three points only the book itself can speak, but I shall comment on the other two.

3.   *Mainstream biblical structuralism*

3.1   Structural exegeses of the Bible inspired by Greimas and Lévi-Strauss have mostly shared the widespread assumption that these two pioneers are reductionists *par excellence*; that they are the authors of a few deductive models of great precision and (claimed) universal application, so that their methods depend on fitting all texts (indeed all human productions) to the models. This perhaps explains the number of exegeses (often good ones, elegant and marked by a sense of discovery) by scholars who never try the method again. If all structural analyses are, in principle, the same, then when you've done one, you've done them all. This view of Greimas and Lévi-Strauss is wrong, or at least much too simple. At their best they show us ways to avoid the reductionism to which structuralism is prone, and encourage us to insist on the specific characteristics of the Bible, rather than suppress them.

3.2   In the case of Greimas, the fault has not been all on the side of his readers, for he did not, either in *Sémantique structurale* (1966) or in *Du sens* (1970), guard himself against the reductionist charge. But such a charge cannot be properly levelled against his later book, *Maupassant* (1976), which is a superb example of the interplay of the deductive and the inductive, of letting the text direct the methods applied to it, as well as of the variety of methods in the literary structuralist's repertoire. The earlier works established his method, and the price that was paid, of giving an unfortunate and wrong impression of the structuralist enterprise, was not too high for the gains he made. But, faced with a real text, in its uniqueness, it is *Maupassant* that I want to have in my hand. In the case of Lévi-Strauss, most of the trouble has stemmed from an absurd emphasis on one single article out of his immense output, 'The Structural Study of Myth' (1963b: 206-31). Important methodological principles are no doubt stated there, but the practical examples consist of a brief *bagatelle* with the Oedipus myth which, despite his disclaimers, remains by far his most influential analysis, and of a few odds and ends from Amerindian mythology. He also, in this article, suggests some deductive models for the understanding of mythic transformations; but these, however useful, certainly do not dominate his serious analysis of myths, particularly his *magnum opus*, the four-volume *Mythologiques* (1970, 1973, 1978, 1981), where he allows his models to become as complicated as they need to be in the face of the massiveness of his chosen object, the entire extant mythology of Indians from one end of the Americas to the other.[1] My superscript to this introduction, from Greimas, seems to me to capture well the disciplined openness of both his method and Lévi-Strauss's.

3.3   Both scholars invite a variety of responses. It not being my way to follow masters closely, I particularly value those who do. The application of a 'pure' Greimasian approach to the Bible continues in the capable hands of Daniel Patte. I have long wished that someone would take on the discipline of a full-scale but 'narrow' Lévi-

Straussian treatment of the Hebrew Bible, a *Mythologiques bibliques*. This has now been brilliantly attempted in a dissertation by the Danish scholar Hans Jorgen Jensen, the early translation of which is much to be desired. But, for myself, I find inspiration in both Greimas and Lévi-Strauss to create stratagems based on theirs, rather than to imitate theirs. There is inspiration, too, in the very scope of the *Mythologiques*. The immensity of the Hebrew Bible makes existing rather atomistic efforts at structural analysis of it, including my own, seem painfully inadequate. But launching oneself into the semantics of the Bible is less ambitious than taking on those of Indian mythology, and Lévi-Strauss gives hope that some control can be achieved of the immensity.

4. *New methodological concerns*

4.1   I find my present work taking two new directions, following two trends which are both well-established in recent scholarship, but which, at least in biblical studies, have remained separate. The first, indeed, has made little impact on biblical studies at all; this is the critical approach most often indicated by the term 'deconstruction' (though other terms, especially the 'indeterminacy' of texts, indicate something similar).[2] Despite the fashionable term 'post-structuralism', deconstruction does not claim simply to supersede structuralism—it *assumes* structuralism, and subverts it from within. The most characteristic move in Derrida is to subvert/cancel/reverse binary oppositions; one can deconstruct only where one has posited structure (for expositions, cf. Culler: 85-89; Ryan: 9-16). On the other hand, as I have argued elsewhere (Jobling, 1979), structuralism has intellectual roots in a 'hermeneutic of suspicion'; to show the structures of sense-making (in a text, for instance) is to show the structures of failing-to-make-sense. Deconstruction depends, then, on structural analysis, and structural analysis tends towards deconstruction.

4.2   The second concern is with the liberation theologies, among which I include feminist theology, and specifically the biblical studies, hermeneutical and exegetical, which they have generated. If there were no other good reason for trying to come to terms with these, working in a North American seminary would suffice! Voices such as those of Elisabeth Schüssler Fiorenza, Norman K. Gottwald, and Fernando Belo are being heard by theological students, and the teaching of the Bible is changing accordingly.

4.3 The precise focus of my coming work will be the problem of the connectedness of these two concerns. Outside of biblical studies, politically engaged writers—Marxists, feminists and others—have been deeply divided (if they have not ignored it altogether) over how to receive deconstruction. Marxists have tended to reject it as an irrelevant bourgeois critical game, though there have been exceptions, while a number of feminists have developed their own consciously deconstructive methods (cf. the discussions in Culler: 156-179, and Ryan, and the feminists mentioned by Showalter: 139). This debate is relevant to the issues in theology and biblical studies. On the one hand, the enterprise in which liberation and feminist theologians are engaged is deconstructive; breaking the 'logic', as well as the overt institutions, of oppression. This is perhaps clearer in feminism, for male *vs.* female has been one of the oppositions most obviously posited in creating a 'logic' for hierarchical social organization (though so has white vs. black, if not quite so pivotally!). Deconstruction provides specific techniques for showing the logic of oppression failing to make sense. On the other hand, as Jonathan Culler puts it, 'Such projects risk bathos—does one need Derrida to unravel the contradictions of right-wing political rhetoric?' (158); and how is one to avoid seeming to offer an 'indeterminate' Bible to those who seek one that is determinate and for their comfort?

4.4 I did not begin any of the studies in this volume with these concerns directly in mind, and am surprised, in retrospect, at the extent of their presence in the finished versions—though often an ambiguous and elusive presence. Chapter 1 is the most clearly deconstructive, attempting to show how, in Gen. 2–3, binary oppositions can be 'established' only by being assumed in advance. When 'male *vs.* female' emerged as one of the most significant of these oppositions, I consciously rewrote the final version as a feminist deconstruction of the text. Chapter 2 raises the political issues, and then, as it seems, confuses them. Its theme, government in Israel, points towards current political theology, but the conclusion, that there is a deep 'indeterminacy' in the Deuteronomic History between pro- and anti-monarchical attitudes, does not seem immediately 'usable'. Chapter 3 can be read as a deconstruction of Israelite attitudes to the question of what land is 'ours' and what 'not ours', and takes something of a feminist turn when it emerges that the logic of the biblical point of view can be made to (seem to) work only by the implicit marginalization of women.

5.   *Technical matters*

5.1   In Volume I it seemed necessary to include an index of technical terms, as a guide for readers to the 'jargon' for which structuralism is famous. Through no particularly conscious attempt, the technical terminology has been much thinned out in Volume II. The terms that occur frequently are the ones that have proved their value, and I shall make a few comments on them here; any other problems of definition can be resolved by reference to Volume I, or, much better, to the dictionary of Greimas and Courtès. *Semantic* and its cognates were always acceptable as normal English, and *synchronic* and *diachronic* seem now to have become so. *Binary oppositions* and their *mediation* define Lévi-Straussian structuralism at its most basic level, so that a familiarity with these terms must be assumed. I have continued to use (I §1.23) the basic schemata of Propp and Greimas. Beyond these, there are just two kinds of terminology which, because of their continuing strangeness and their prevalence here, require some comment.

5.2   An essential part of each of these studies is *isotopic analysis*, a technique which I find invariably useful. An *isotopy*, as I use the term, is 'a semantic category defined broadly enough to subsume a large number of elements of meaning in the text, but precisely enough for useful organization of these elements' (adapted from Jobling, 1984: 201). This is a pragmatic rather than a strict definition, and I believe the use of the technique will speak for itself. I prefer 'isotopy' to 'code', from which it does not greatly differ in meaning (cf. Greimas, 1966: 69-70; 1970: 189-97; Lévi-Strauss, 1970: 199).

5.3   I use in a somewhat special way the opposition (derived from linguistics) 'paradigmatic' *vs.* 'syntagmatic' analysis. These terms will appear in every study, but particularly importantly in the last, where I consciously adopt and compare approaches which differ on the paradigmatic-syntagmatic scale. In using the terms, I assume that the object of analysis is *narrative*. All the studies are in what Freedman (226) calls the 'Primary Narrative' (Genesis to 2 Kings—excluding Ruth—a single sequential narrative covering close to half of the Hebrew Bible; clearly much material not originally narrative has gone into its making, but this material has been 'narratized' by its very incorporation). By paradigmatic analysis, I mean taking sections of the biblical text which stand in some significant relation to each other (detaching them initially from context) and comparing them in parallel. The innumerable pieces of which the Primary Narrative is made are often loosely connected, and their susceptibility to fruitful treatment in detachment from their narrative context is clear from historical-critical research (especially form-criticism). Ultimately, however, they have not reached us as separate entities, but in a sequential arrangement—not merely as texts, but as *a text*[3]—and the constraints of this 'narratization' must be accounted for in any adequate structural approach. By syntagmatic analysis, therefore, I mean working out the significance of the order in which the sections appear (and of what, if anything, comes between them). In working out analytic strategies to integrate the two phases, I find that one is generally on one's own. Lévi-Strauss's work on myths is suggestive for the paradigmatic phase, but (since he deals normally with separate entities which come in no sequence) he has nothing to offer for the syntagmatic. In principle, Greimas supplies the lack; but in fact his techniques are of limited usefulness in dealing with so immense a sequence as the Primary Narrative. My normal approach is paradigmatic followed by syntagmatic analysis, though in particular cases the order of the steps may be reversed. A special case, to which I sometimes refer, is that of 'enclosing' and 'enclosed' narratives (Vol. I/3 for a case-study), that is, the relationship between a piece of narrative and another narrative which surrounds it.

5.4   I have retained the system of decimal paragraph numbers. They indicate the hierarchical organization of each chapter, and attention to them will facilitate the reading. A zero in this system always implies *introductory* comments, even when this is not specifically stated. The numbers provide for cross-referencing within a chapter; between chapters the chapter number precedes the decimal paragraph number (e.g. 2 §1.231); and back to Volume I, by means of a slash (e.g. Vol. I/2 §1.231). To minimize footnotes, references to secondary literature are included in the text, and can be unambiguously determined by reference to the list of 'Works Consulted'.

The Structuralist Exegesis Seminar of the SBL has continued to provide a context for my work, and in particular I thank Gary Phillips and Hugh White for good conversations. Norman Gottwald has tried to see the point even when it was not clear to me. I thank the faculty and students of St. Andrew's College for support and stimulation, and my family for the privations they have borne. The members of the Department of Biblical Studies at the University of Sheffield, aside from being my publishers, have shown me unfailing hospitality, and given me the benefit of invaluable discussion, during a summer in Sheffield (when Chapter 3 was born) and now during a sabbatical year. To them this book is dedicated.

Chapter 1

MYTH AND ITS LIMITS IN GENESIS 2.4b–3.24

In the same way that the Greek archaic society would have been unable to decide whether man was autochthonous or born from two parents, the Hebrew archaic society would have hesitated between two opposite appraisals of man's condition. In both cases, a myth would arise as an attempt to unconsciously find a way out of an impasse by substituting the level of artistic creativity to that of logic (Casalis, 1976: 49).

Our literature neither leaves women alone nor allows them to participate (Fetterley, 1978: xii).

0. *Introduction*

0.0 The biblical section before us has attracted a great deal of structural analysis. One reason, of course, is its intrinsic importance— what kind of analysis has it not attracted, over the centuries? It is in some way basic to the Bible, and advocates of new approaches want to try their hand at it. But beyond this general reason, there is certainly a sense that structural methods are particularly appropriate here. Structural methods have been applied with special intensity to the study of *myth*, and the beginning of Genesis is, in some sense, myth. It is not, therefore, surprising that the members of the Seminar on Structural Exegesis at the Society of Biblical Literature took Genesis 2.4b–3.24 as the object of their first set of comparative structural readings. The results are collected in *Semeia* 18, edited by Daniel Patte. It was there that the first version of the present chapter appeared, in a very compressed form, and the contributions of my colleagues to that volume form an important part of the context of this new version—I have refined and redefined my positions in response to them.

0.11   It was not long after the appearance of Lévi-Strauss's seminal essay, 'The Structural Study of Myth', that Edmund Leach initiated, in two celebrated articles, the mythic analysis of Genesis by Lévi-Straussian methods (Lévi-Strauss, 1963b: 206-31; Leach, 1961, 1969: 7-23). However, in the context of a debate with Paul Ricoeur, Lévi-Strauss himself responded sceptically to Leach's work. The key passage in his response is this:

> ... the Old Testament, which certainly puts to use mythic materials, borrows them with a different goal in mind from their original one. The redactors, without a doubt, have deformed them in interpreting them; that is, these myths have been submitted ... to an intellectual operation (1963a: 631-32).

As best I understand Lévi-Strauss (though I do not know that he has himself used the analogy)[1], myth in primitive societies, that is, societies which have not developed a historical consciousness, is analogous to 'free association' in psychoanalysis. Such societies express their sense of the world by using the elements of experience, combining them and opposing them in ways which seem appropriate (combining jaguars with cooking-fire, for example, or opposing honey to tobacco) unconstrained by any sense of need for historical or scientific coherence. Such totally free association is, no doubt, an ideal concept, but Lévi-Strauss's work depends on this ideal's being approached; the *vigour* of myths depends on the freedom of association. As historical consciousness develops, 'the mythic substance allows its internal principles of organization to seep away. Its structural content is diminished. Whereas at the beginning the transformations were vigorous, by the end they became quite feeble' (1978: 129). Myth turns into consciously achieved literature.

0.12   Leach later rejected Lévi-Strauss's misgivings (1969: 25-31), but his arguments do not appear to me really to get at Lévi-Strauss's point, and his procedure in relation to Genesis seems indeed not sufficiently to allow for the differences between such a literary text and the myths of pre-historical societies. He affirms in the early chapters of Genesis a clear and vigorous set of mythic oppositions. He appears to be on strong ground in Gen. 1.1–2.4a, for the first creation account is indeed constructed as a system of oppositions (though, if this text were the object of my present investigation, I would press the question whether these oppositions are not rather proto-scientific than mythic, and therefore in need of a different kind of treatment). But Gen. 2.4b–3.24 is a very different kind of text, and Leach's reduction of its literary complexity to a few basic oppositions is cavalier (Leach, 1969: 13-15; for other critiques of Leach on Genesis, cf. the references in White, 1979: 50-51, and especially Carroll).

0.13   I agree with Lévi-Strauss that his methods cannot be applied to the Israelite myths in such a direct way. But he did not, apparently, want to close the door entirely to a more nuanced application, for he adds the following to his remark quoted above: 'It would be necessary to begin with a preliminary task, aimed at recovering the mythological and archaic residue underlying the biblical literature, which obviously could be the work only of a specialist' (1963a: 632). It is from this point that I have begun the following analysis; for it seems to me that Gen. 2.4b–3.24 may provide a textbook example of myth in the process of becoming literature. The structure of mythic opposition is not fully clear in this text, but it is sufficiently clear to convince me, at least, of a mythic substrate. There is demanded a 'preliminary task'. Or perhaps we should rather say, a redefinition of the total interpretive task, conformable to the nature of this particular text. We need not only to discover the underlying mythic oppositions, but also to give an account of how and why they have become unclear in the text we have; and to do all of this with the literary finesse demanded by the text's complexity.

0.2   My analysis has been prepared, then, in the context of ongoing discussion of biblical structural exegesis, particularly in relation to parts of the Bible which are in some sense mythic. But there is a second context, that of feminist exegesis. Gen. 2.4b–3.24 is, of course, a text to which feminist scholars have given much attention; foremost among their exegeses is that of Trible (72-143). Her conclusions diverge completely from mine, because she views the nature of the text differently, and the issues between us seem to me to be of quite basic importance for the programme of feminist biblical exegesis. Believing this programme to be one of the most important aspects of current biblical scholarship, and believing also that structural methods of exegesis have a potential, almost wholly unexploited, for furthering that programme, I have concluded my analysis with a brief examination of the exegetical and interpretive issues involved.

1. Narrative Analysis

1.0   How is the narrative shape of the text before us to be perceived as a whole? I shall begin by pointing to the weaknesses of the narrative model which comes first to mind, that of 'creation and fall'. I shall then develop an alternative model, that of 'a man to till the earth', which avoids these weaknesses, but proves to have others of a different kind. The text is in tension between these two models.

1.1   The model 'Creation and fall'

1.11   The narrative model normally proposed for Genesis 2.4b–3.24 is that of 'creation and fall', with a certain freedom in the delineation of each and in the determination of their relation to each other. This proposal is usually made without close consideration of the issues of narrative analysis. But even an analysis like that of Culley (1980), which considers the narrative issues very deeply, seems to me to fit within the 'creation and fall' model. In criticizing this model, I shall have Culley's treatment particularly in mind.

1.12   The *fall* is the less problematic element. This theme clearly comprehends the whole of 3.1-19, up to the end of the divine curses. 3.20-21 is obscurely related to the fall, but may imply coming to terms with, and provision for, fallen existence. 3.22-24 depends on the fall, and even carries the theme further; but it has a curious quality of afterthought—does the expulsion really add anything to the curses? To the fall theme belongs also 2.16-17 (which in turn depends on 2.9). *Creation* proves more difficult, but as an initial suggestion it may be perceived in two stages: the creation of 'man'[2] and vegetation in mutual dependence, with water as an important third term in their relationship (2.5-15), and the creation of animals and woman (2.18-25). The two stages are separated by the prohibition in 2.16-17.

1.13   Culley's analysis falls within the scope of these initial remarks (for the following, Culley: 28-32). In 2.16-17, 3.1-19 he essentially finds the fall sequence, which he regards as the *main* sequence in the whole text (though he elaborates the discussion by separating from the human fall the theme of the fault and punishment of the serpent). He does not treat 3.20-21, and perceives 3.22-24 as dependent on the fall, though in no clear logical relation to it. He defines 2.4b-25 as a whole as the creation sequence (without commenting on the odd role of 2.16-17 within it), but he treats 2.18-25 separately, as an 'embedded sequence' with its own agenda.

1.14   Culley is well aware of the difficulty of defining, within such a 'creation and fall' model, the precise relationship between the two elements. The fall is certainly dominant, and in principle the creation sequence merely provides background information for it. But the creation account is more elaborate than one would expect for this purpose—it develops interests independent of the fall sequence— which Culley can only explain by suggesting that this creation account once existed independently of the fall narrative. But the difficulties surely do not end here. The 'creation' evoked in Gen. 2 does not have the expected comprehensiveness. While accepting that it eschews a taxonomic approach (contrast Gen. 1) in favour of narrative tension (the earth's need for water, the man's need for a helper), one still expects some account of the creation of heavenly bodies (especially in view of 'the earth and the heavens', 2.4b). There is no expression of the *completeness* of creation at the end of the sequence (contrast 2.1-3). The possibility arises that the creation sequence has been attenuated by the dominance of the fall sequence. The culmination of Culley's careful analysis is a 'creation and fall' model in which the creation element hovers awkwardly between subordination to the fall in some respects, and surprising independence in others.

1.151   But the issues must be pressed even harder. It seems to me that there are two main features of our text which the 'creation and fall' model cannot explain at all. The first is the narrative function of 2.18-25. In itself, it appears to be an element in a creation sequence (though one could imagine it as something else than this, since it has its own independent themes). In its present context, however, it has become indispensable to the fall sequence *within* which it is found. The point becomes clear if we consider what the effect would be of reversing 2.16-17 and 2.18-25—something which it seems could be done very easily. The creation sequence would proceed without interruption, and would as a whole precede the fall sequence; humanity in its fulness would exist before there was any thought of fall. And the prohibition of 2.16-17 would naturally then be addressed to *both* man and woman (in line with what we actually find suggested in 3.1-5). The existing order, on the other hand, surely goes out of its way to stress that it is the *man's* fate alone which is at issue in 2.16-17, but that, since the serpent and the woman will be essential actors in the working out of it, their existence must be accounted for before the fall story can proceed. (The centrality of the man does not end here—though the serpent and the woman will be involved in the curses, only the man will be expelled from the garden in 3.22-24.) The creation interest of 2.18-25 has been much more radically subordinated to the fall than an analysis like Culley's allows; yet 2.18-25 also resists being interpreted *merely* as a means of acquiring the *dramatis personae* of the following section.

1.152   The second inexplicable feature is the *garden*, that is, the spatial distinction between the earth as a whole and the special garden which God plants (2.5-9). This distinction is disruptive of the creation sequence, and not accountable in its terms. What does the creation of a garden have to do with the making of 'the earth and the heavens'? Most of 'creation' took place, it seems, *inside* the garden, and providing it with a special water supply takes up an inordinate proportion of a brief creation account (2.10-14)! But the garden theme is in some tension also with the fall sequence. The expulsion with which our text ends (3.22-24) depends again on the garden/whole earth distinction (not only in the obvious spatial sense, but also in the necessity of separating the man from the tree of life which is in the garden; 3.22, cf. 2.9). Yet, as suggested above, the expulsion comes anticlimactically after the comprehensive punishments in the fall sequence proper (3.14-19), which indicate nothing of the spatial distinction.

1.16   Culley claims that his model presents our text as a unity (Culley: 28, 32), but I do not believe that it can be unified by means of this or any other 'creation and fall' model. Little is left of 'creation' if the 'garden' material is not relevant to it, and if the relevance even of 2.18-25 is dubious; and the 'fall', while clearly the dominant theme, also leaves the 'garden' material unexplained, and comprehends 2.18-25 at best oddly. There is room to ask whether any other narrative model is available.

1.2   *The model 'A man to till the earth'*[3]

1.21   Narratives generally move from a statement of problems to the resolution of the problems. The beginning of our present text (2.5) is marked by a series of lacks in the newly-created earth:

1. no vegetation,
2. no rain,
3. no man to till the ground.

The first lack is a consequence of the other two. How does the following narrative resolve them? First, the lack of rain receives an ambiguous response in 2.6—is this mist thought of as supplying adequate moisture? Then, in 2.7, a man is created. Have the conditions for vegetation now been met? Yes, for Yahweh is able to plant a garden (2.8-9), which, after further attention to its water supply (2.10-14), the man begins to till (2.15). At first sight, 2.4b-15 provides an excellently self-contained sequence.

1.22 But there arises the problem, previously alluded to, of the separation between the whole earth and the garden. The initial lacks are *defined* in terms of the whole earth, but are *resolved* almost exclusively in terms of the garden: 1. we hear of the vegetation only in the garden; the earth's water supply remains ambiguous—it has the 'mist' but, despite the broad geographical reference of 2.11-14, the river of 2.10 exists specifically 'to water the garden'; 3. it is the garden that the man is set to till (2.8, 15).[4] In this connection, 3.23 demands an attention which it has rarely received (but cf. Naidoff), for it resolves the whole earth–garden issue, and fulfills the *original* lacks, in the most precise terms. The man is expelled from the garden, reversing his introduction into it (2.8, 15). He is sent 'to till the ground from which he was taken'—taken (2.7) before his introduction into the garden—and this new task is plainly something different from tilling the garden (2.15). A profound link between the beginning and end of our text is confirmed by other considerations. The expulsion of the man alone, where we expect mention of the woman, confirms the link to the initial situation in which the man is alone. The expulsion, which appeared redundant in relation to the fall theme (§1.152), is essential in relation to the earth's original lack. And the tree of life, forgotten since its appearance in 2.9, becomes a concern again in 3.22. Only in relation to the theme of water does a certain tension remain in my proposed scheme of the fulfilment at the end of the text of the lacks stated at the beginning. Vegetation requires water as well as manpower. The garden has enjoyed rich vegetation, but we have not heard of the earth's having any—what, then, can the man expect as he begins to till it? But this tension is not great—we are surely to suppose that, since the earth has some sort of water supply (the mist, at least), it can produce some sort of vegetation under tillage. This agrees with conditions of *hard* agriculture evoked in the curse of 3.17-19, a connection which I shall explore below.

1.231   The beginning and end of our text are the beginning and end of a narrative programme—to get 'a man to till the earth'. Such a programme can be presented by means of the now familiar 'actantial schema' of Greimas (1966: 172-91).

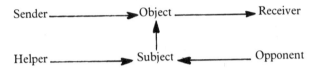

The six elements are called actants, and need not be persons. The *sender* brings the action about, with the aim of getting the *object* to the *receiver*. The *subject* is the protagonist of the action, and is aided and opposed by various *helpers* and *opponents*. In the present case, the *object* is 'a man', and the receiver is 'the earth'. But how are we to define the other actants? I believe that we can be assisted in this further determination of the narrative programme by an analysis employing the scheme of Propp (1968:25-65), and oddly reminiscent of the one I proposed in 'Ahab's Quest for Rain' (I/3 §1.2), with the same kind of reversal of expected roles; an analysis capable of providing an initial, though not yet adequate, account of the middle of our text (2.16–3.21), as well as of its beginning and end.

> *Initial situation* (2.4b-7). Through a brief narrative an apparently satisfactory situation is evoked. The earth, which lacked water and a farmer, has received both (though the adequacy of the water supply is unclear).
> *Villainy* (2.8-15). Yahweh, in the role of villain, steals the man from the earth to work his own private domain (the garden). He also provides the garden with water, and luxuriant vegetation fills it.
> *Counteraction and combat* (2.16–3.7). The process whereby the villainy is reversed is most complex, and I shall for now defer many details. But the starting-point has to be 2.16-17. There is

a flaw in the villain's plan—if the man eats of a certain tree in the garden, the villain will lose his hold on him (cf. 3.22-23!). The villain therefore defends this tree with a threat. The counteraction must, then, consist of getting the man to eat of the forbidden tree; the serpent, the woman, and the man himself eventually accomplish this. The main combat, unusually, does not require the villain's presence—Yahweh is represented, in 3.1-7, by his prohibition, and it is this which is 'defeated'. When Yahweh arrives on the scene, the combat is over.

Marking of the hero (3.8-19). As frequently in the Proppian tale, the most the villain can do is to leave his mark on the one/ones who has/have defeated him. The curses fulfil this feature; they fall upon the serpent, the woman, and the man.

The hero's return home (3.22-24). The effect of the expulsion is that the man returns from the scene of combat (the garden) to his initial place (the earth), an odd but exact example of this Proppian feature. It may be added that the *marriage*, in which the Proppian tale characteristically ends, appears in 4.1, which, however, has become part of a new story; 3.20-21, which is hard to place narratively, may be related to the marriage theme.

1.2321 Two major issues arise from this analysis.[5] The first is the role of Yahweh as villain, which is the keystone of the entire analysis. Though a few features of the text support this role-assignment—in 3.8 Yahweh is found using the garden for private pleasure, and in 3.22-23 he appears threatened by the man, even fearing that he may lose control of the garden—nonetheless Yahweh as villain is obviously an idea alien to the *surface* level of our text. Indeed, Yahweh seems in several ways to occupy the opposite role. It is he who creates the man initially within the context of the earth's need (though this *might* be interpreted narratively as a deception, to cloak the real use he has in mind for the man). In 3.23, it is apparently Yahweh's *intention* that the man should till the earth after the expulsion. Yahweh makes some provision for the humans even after his 'defeat' (3.21).

1.2322 The ambiguity of Yahweh lies above all in his originating the counteraction against his own villainy. He is, indeed, himself responsible for the flaw in his plan, for it is he who inexplicably plants the tree of knowledge; nonetheless, by 2.17 the villain's plan seems to have succeeded—the man is tilling the garden, and even the danger from the tree has been neutralized by the prohibition. It is in

2.18-25 that the villain most conspicuously undermines his own interests, in creating first the animals and then the woman. Why was it 'not good that the man should be alone' (2.18)? The text does not suggest that he was complaining, or that Yahweh was dissatisfied with his work! It is precisely out of this initiative by Yahweh that the counteraction develops, for its agents are the serpent—one of the animals—and the woman. In sum, the same character Yahweh invests the Greimasian roles of *sender* and *opponent*, a mark of a profoundly ambiguous text.[6]

1.2323   The second issue concerns the remaining Greimasian roles, of subject and helper. The obvious investments, the man as subject, the serpent and the woman as helper, are complicated by our Proppian analysis. It is true that it is in the person of the man that the earth is to get its tiller, and eventually does; again we recall that the woman disappears at the end (3.22-24). But, on the other hand, *responsibility* for the counteraction lies much more with the serpent and the woman than with the man; they, more than he, resemble the Proppian hero. The man, it is true, does to some extent participate in the counteraction—not only in choosing to eat the fruit, but also in his active collaboration in the creation of the animals and the woman—but on the whole, he is a profoundly passive character throughout the story. It is the serpent and the woman who heroically oppose Yahweh the villain, and it is very significant that they share with the man the important Proppian function of the *marking* of the hero (the curses of 3.14-19). We perhaps must think of the Greimasian subject not as the man, but as 'humanity' (both sexes), or even humanity and animals together (the *living* creation; cf. 'all living' in 3.20—*kl-ḥy*, punning not only on 'Eve', *ḥwh*, but also on 'animals', *ḥyym*). What we then do with the 'helper' role is not important, though 'the serpent's cunning' would be a good candidate.

1.233   I propose, then, the following actantial scheme for 'getting a man to till the earth':

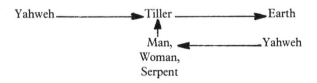

Yahweh ⟶ Tiller ⟶ Earth

Man, ⟵ Yahweh
Woman,
Serpent

Further discussion of this scheme will be deferred for the semantic analysis.

1.3   *The tension between the models*

1.31   A narrative model for our text based on 'a man to till the earth' unifies the text in a way that a 'creation and fall' model can not. But merely to replace the latter with the former is quite unsatisfactory. For the 'creation and fall' model—or the 'fall' model as I shall from now on call it, because of the subordination of the creation element— is much closer to the superficial narrative interest of the text. If one were to ask the average person literate in the Bible what happens in Gen. 2–3, the answer would probably be 'the fall' and 'the origin of sexuality and marriage' (i.e. 2.18-25), in that order of importance. No one senses that the text is about enabling vegetation by finding a gardener! Our text presents us with a paradox at the narrative level. By the usual criteria of closure of incident, appearance of one limited group of characters, and clear separation from material preceding and following, Gen. 2.4b–3.24 is a unit, and one expects thematic unity. But its major theme does not (or its major themes do not) unify it—rather it is unified by a superficially minor theme. The programme 'a man to till the earth' has been overtaken or 'upstaged' by other themes—especially the theological theme of the fall, and to a smaller extent the social theme of marriage—which have captured the narrative interest.[7]

1.32   Within the 'fall' model, the text has the form of a *myth*, a transformation from 'before' to 'after', with, in this case, 'before' valued positively, and 'after' negatively. Within the model of 'a man to till the earth', the text has the form of a *folk-tale*, with movement from order to disorder to order reestablished (cf. Propp), which suggests the valuing of the final (= initial) situation of order. The paradox of the text is that we have a folk-tale subverted by a myth (because of the 'upstaging' just referred to) *and* subverting the myth (because of the greater unifying power of the folk-tale model). Our analysis must account for this paradox.

2.   *Semantic analysis*

2.01   Our text creates two opposed 'logics' of human existence, each, so far as may be, self-consistent. In terms of the narrative model of the fall, they are the logics of 'before' and 'after', but in terms of the narrative model of 'a man to till the earth', they are the logics of 'inside' and 'outside' the garden. I shall choose one terminology or the other according to the model under consideration at each stage of analysis; but shall prefer that of 'inside' *vs.* 'outside', because the folk-tale model better comprehends the whole text. Though it is the narrative analysis which has suggested these opposed logics, or *semantic configurations*, semantic analysis will not correspond to narrative segmentation; for example, the data for the logic of 'outside' will not be drawn only from the parts of the narrative set outside the garden. Elements belonging to the logic of 'outside' or 'after' have invaded the narrative of 'inside' or 'before'. The reason why this *must* be so will appear later (§2.2), but a single example may be given here. In 3.17-19, the man is condemned to hard labour, and his eventual death is referred to. Narratively, this occurs at an ambiguous point in the story—after the fall but before the departure from the garden. But the conditions described in 3.17-19 belong necesssarily to the semantics of 'outside'; for the man's death, as we learn later, will be *outside* the garden—indeed, the reason for his expulsion (3.22) is that he might otherwise *avoid* his death (cf. Culley: 29, 'the difficult conditions described seem to be what would apply outside the garden rather than inside it'). The oppositions I shall propose will, rather, be established logically. Leach speaks of the characteristic work of myth as the positing of 'another world' in opposition to the world of experience, so that 'the attributes of this other world are necessarily those which are not of this world' (1969: 10). I shall postulate a set of attributes in respect of which 'this world' is the reverse of the 'other world' in Gen. 2.4b–3.24, and test the value of the model against the text itself.

2.02   First, I shall exhibit the opposed semantic configurations under various semantic fields or *isotopies* (Introduction §5.2), and show to what extent the text can be organized under them (§2.1). Then I shall explore the way the myth of the 'fall' has worked with these oppositions, and, in particular, 'mediated' them (§2.2). Finally, I shall consider the new perspective in which this mythic work appears when the text is looked at under the model of 'a man to till the earth' (§2.3).

2.1 *The semantic configurations of 'inside' and 'outside'*

2.10 The following table summarizes the configurations, and the isotopies under which I shall present them:

	'Inside'	'Outside'
Isotopy of culture	Easy agriculture Agriculture only No animals	Hard agriculture (Agriculture and husbandry/hunting) Animals
Isotopy of society and sexuality	Solitariness Male only Autochthony	Society Male and female Sexual generation
Isotopy of vitality	Immortality	Mortality
Isotopy of Knowledge	Ignorance	Knowledge

The semantics of 'inside' is manifested almost—but not quite—perfectly in 2.4b-15. 'Humanity' is a solitary male, born autochthonously, and immortal. His business is agriculture, which is easy for him; there are no animals nor need of them. The man is ignorant of these conditions of his existence (i.e., that there might be alternatives). The semantics of 'outside' is unambiguous from 3.7 onward. Humanity is two sexes in society, born sexually, and mortal. Its business is still largely agriculture, but this is now hard; indeed hardness dominates the respective lives of both sexes. Animals exist, and even share the hardness of life; culture based on animals (hunting, husbandry) exists alongside agriculture (because of the hardness of the latter?). Humanity knows these conditions of its existence, and can posit alternatives. Elements of both semantics occur in 2.16–3.6, for reasons to be considered (§2.2).

2.11 *The isotopy of culture*

2.111 Throughout the text, the man's vocation is agriculture. His essential relationship is with the soil (cf. the etymological relation between *'dm*, 'man', and *'dmh*, 'ground'); he comes from it, lives off it, is responsible for it, and his death is defined as a return to it. It is as a mere predicate of the earth's needs that he is first introduced (2.4b-7), and the curse upon him (3.17-19) has to do entirely with his relationship to *it* (and not, remarkably, to the woman or the animals). 'Inside' and 'outside' are defined for him as divergent possibilities for his relationship to the earth—ease or hardship. This opposition is supported by a subordinate one, that of *wet vs. dry*. Moisture in the text is relevant only to the conditions of agriculture. 'Inside', there is a special, copious water supply (2.10-14). 'Outside', the supply is unsatisfactory (vv. 5-6), and this dryness of the earth is stressed in the curse on the man ('thorns and thistles', 3.18).[8]

2.112 'Inside', there are no animals. Our text says virtually nothing about how they participate in the conditions of 'outside'—the curse on the serpent is a special case whose point lies elsewhere. But it is striking that Yahweh clothes the man and the woman for the 'outside' with *skins*, an animal product (they themselves having used *leaves* for the purpose; 3.21, cf. 3.7). This is the only hint of the cultural *use* of animals; it is to be noted, however, that the very next pericope, 4.1-16, makes such culture central.

2.12   *The isotopy of society and sexuality*

2.121 'Inside', woman does not exist—the solitary 'earth-creature' is male (against Trible: 80; cf. §3.12). 'Outside', she shares the hardness of life, indeed has more than her share of it. But this hardness is defined for her wholly in terms of her sexual/generative function; it includes being subordinated to the will of the man (3.16). She possesses, indeed, a dignity, but this also is defined in sexual/generative terms: she is to be 'the mother of all living' (3.20).

2.122   This last reference recalls the link between the woman and the animals noted above in the narrative analysis (§1.2323). This link is strong throughout the text. The woman first appears in the same category as the animals, that of potential 'helper' for the man (2.18-25). In 3.1-5, it is to her that the serpent has direct access, and we find a threefold repetition of the sequence serpent–woman–man (or *vice versa*) in 3.1-6, 8-13, and 14-19, suggesting 'woman' as a mediating category between 'man' and 'animals' (cf. Leach, 1969: 14); and something similar is suggested by the theme of the man's naming of animals and woman (for which see §2.226). Though there are complicating elements to which we shall have to return, *one* of the dynamics of our text is to set 'man' over against 'woman and animals'.

2.13 *The isotopies of life and knowledge: the two trees*

2.1311 The curse on the man refers to his mortality—'till you return to the ground' (3.19). There is no superficial justification for reading 2.17 as 'You shall become mortal', but semantic coherence demands this view. In the absence of sexuality, human continuance depends on immortality; it is essential to the logic of 'inside'.[9] The little we are told of the tree of life entirely fits this picture. Eating of it brings *eternal* life, according to 3.22. It was present inside the garden (2.9), and not forbidden to the man (2.16-17). It is not said that he actually ate of it—this would create narrative difficulty since it would mean that he had gained immortality indelibly—but the situation can be translated mythically as 'immortality belonged to the man inside the garden'. Only *after* his eating of the tree of knowledge does it become necessary to keep him from eating of the tree of life.

2.1312 A famous *crux interpretum* is the death sentence of 2.17, which is *not* later carried out. The clear literal implication of this verse is that the man will die *immediately* upon eating the fruit. But, again, we are obliged to translate it mythically as 'in the day that you eat of it you will become mortal' (cf. Crossan: 109-10). For the man's instant death at 3.6 would leave no space for a new solution to the problem of human continuity—there would be nowhere for the myth to go, and no 'explanation' of the present human situation. The wording of 3.3 perhaps gives some further support to this line of interpretation: 'You shall not eat of the fruit . . . lest you die' does not *necessarily* imply instant death. Perhaps the words of the 'villain' in 2.17 are an understandable hyperbole!

2.132 Nothing could be clearer than that our text tells of a gain of knowledge by the man (or by humanity), implying that initially, 'inside', he lacked knowledge. It is the tree of knowledge which is forbidden him, and of which he eats (or they eat). Immediately 'they knew' (3.7), and Yahweh later confesses that 'the man has become like one of us, knowing good and evil' (v. 22). Wherein this knowledge precisely consists, the text does not specify. It is arbitrary of Leach

(1969: 14) to identify it with 'knowledge of sexual differentiation', though this, certainly, is one aspect of it. In terms of mythic logic it seems to me best defined as knowledge of the conditions of existence 'outside', and knowledge that this existence is different from the life 'inside' which has been lost. It has even been suggested that 'the curses (*sc.* of 3.14-19) represent the actual content of (the) divine knowledge— man now knows fully what is in store for him' (Naidoff: 10).

2.2   The 'fall' model and a 'middle' semantics

2.211   In relation to the narrative model of the 'fall', Gen. 2.4b–3.24 appears as a typical myth of transformation, from 'other world' to 'this world', from 'before' to 'after'. I have suggested the mythic logics of these opposed worlds by the series of specific oppositions enumerated in §2.1. The obvious problem arises, to which we turn in the present section, that certain of these oppositions ('no animals' *vs.* 'animals', 'male only' *vs.* 'male and female') diverge startlingly from the worlds of 'before' and 'after' in the manifest text. But two comments are in order before we take up this issue. First, it *is* in terms of such radical oppositions that myth works—it makes such possibilities *available to thought*; as Leach (1969: 14) remarks, 'In Eden, Adam *can* exist by himself' (my emphasis), i.e. it is *thinkable* in mythic logic. Second, what can we say about the cultural mindset which, through its myth, thinks the oppositions I have posited? It is a mindset, I suggest, which resonates to the appeal of *ease*, in the face of the pains and hardships of experience; but also to the appeal of *simplicity*, indeed the utmost simplicity thinkable, in the face of the complexities of experience. Further, its assumptions are *agricultural* and *male-centred* ('patriarchal', to use the term current in recent feminism, even misogynistic). The complexity of human culture is reduced to the single term of agriculture, perceived no doubt as the most basic aspect of the interaction between humanity and its environment; an agriculture, furthermore, without hardship. The complexity of human society is removed at a stroke—sexual differentiation is perceived as the basis of this complexity, and it can be thought away. Perhaps above all, the complexity of thought itself is removed; the final simplicity is ignorance—not to know, not to be obliged to work things out from a complex range of possibilities.[10] This, as it were, is the ground that myth stakes out in our text.

2.212 But it is ground that the myth cannot hold. There is an inherent problem in myths of transformation; if the 'before' situation was logically consistent, then nothing within it could precipitate its transformation. The more successfully the myth posits two opposed logics, the less it can logically explain how one gave place to the other. Some aspects of 'after' must therefore be permitted to exist within the situation of 'before', in order to precipitate the transformation; but they must be well-concealed if the myth is to have the plausibility to function in a society. It is from the need to conceal or displace its unavoidable points of illogicality that myth gains its creative energy (cf. Lévi-Strauss, 1970: 2-14). Hence what we find manifest in our text is a 'middle' semantics, which mediates, in certain respects, the two semantic configurations posited in §2.1, but which can be made to appear not *essentially* different from the semantics of 'before'. Most of the data appear in the central section of our text, 2.16–3.6; up to 2.15, as we have seen, the logic of 'before' is maintained almost intact (but cf. §2.231), and from 3.7 the logic of 'after' is fully established. I shall present the data according to the isotopies previously introduced.

2.22 *The isotopies of culture and of society and sexuality*

2.221 The presence of animals in our text ought at first sight to come under the isotopy of culture, for there is a natural parallel between the culture of plants and that of animals (including the exploitation of *wild* animals by hunting). But while the former is a central concern of our text, the latter is marginal—there is nothing of the *use* of animals beside the mention of the use of their skins for clothing (3.21). This is in contrast to surrounding material (1.26-30; 4.1-16) which takes an interest in the culture of animals, including the issue of eating them. When animals appear in our present text, it is rather in relation to the theme of *society*—they are created to ease the man's solitude, though they fail to meet this need. There proves to be a close connection between the way the myth works with the animals and the way it works with the woman, so that it is best to treat both in the same section.

2.222 'It is not good that the man should be alone' (2.18). It is here that the middle semantics announces itself most flagrantly and most plausibly. 'Before', there is the male alone, born autochthonously;

'after', there are male and female, and hence a society born sexually. The woman represents the *possibility* of the 'after' situation, and it is therefore natural that she should precipitate the transformation from 'before' to 'after'. But for this purpose she must be introduced into 'before', and this illogical operation is performed as painlessly as her extraction from the man's flesh! That the man's solitude is 'not good' is, as we have seen, a unilateral affirmation by Yahweh, based on nothing that has gone before (and, in fact, incompatible with his previous 'villainy'). But companionship appeals to a basic human sentiment, so that it is more readily overlooked that the creation of the woman destroys the logic of 'before'. Her creation is, furthermore, so presented as not to disturb human *unity*—no sooner are the man and the woman two that they are pronounced 'one flesh'—which helps establish the innocence of the mythic strategem. But, in fact, the man and the woman are not a unity—the story immediately records the woman's *independent* action (3.1-6).

2.223   But the job is far from done! In the 'after' situation, the woman not only *exists* as the guarantee of renewable life, but also *suffers* subordination to the man, based on sexual desire (3.16). To make this situation appear logical, she must not only be introduced into 'before', but must also be made to do there something *worse* that what the man did. This worse thing, which justifies her severer punishment, was to *instigate* the man to his disobedience. I have demonstrated elsewhere a deeply-rooted biblical pattern in which the instigators of sin are more negatively assessed, and more severely punished, than the sinners themselves (Vol. I/Postscript §2.12). Here, the man admittedly ate the fruit, but he would not have done so had it not been for the woman.

2.224   Much, then, has been achieved by having the woman present before the transformation. The one whose existence is necessary to the configuration of 'after' has been introduced into the configuration of 'before', and in a way which justifies her sexually-based subordination. Not to be overlooked in this connection is the non-narrative commentary of 2.24. In the 'after' configuration, the woman is to experience sexuality—childbirth and conjugal desire—in a 'fallen' way, as opposed, we must assume, to some previous 'unfallen' sexuality. But what was this unfallen sexuality? Childbirth has not been mentioned in the previous narrative, and sexual desire has been only hinted at (2.23), and that on the side of the man; logically so, for sexuality has no logical place in the 'before' configuration. But 2.24 'innocently' introduces the ideas of parenthood and sexual mutuality into the story of the 'unfallen' state, as though these things were the presupposition of the myth (belonging to 'before'), rather than its *results* (belonging to 'after')!

2.225 A text omitting the animal theme, and particularly the serpent—such a text would consist of 2.18, 21-25, and 3.6-12—would fully achieve the creation of this 'middle' semantics in respect of the woman. But perhaps it would do so too crassly—the transition from the euphoria of 2.23-25 to the woman's fall in 3.6a would be very sharp. Such a myth would perhaps fall short of plausibility; perhaps there is needed another level of complication, even of obfuscation. In particular, another 'villain'. This is what the creation of the animals provides, and again the stratagem is carried through in all innocence. What could be more natural than that the man in the garden had the animals about him; their presence there is less obtrusive, if less thrilling, that that of the woman! This naturalness no doubt helps disguise the fact that the creation of the animals in our text is purely gratuitous. If the creation of the woman answered a dubious need, at least it *did* answer it. The animals establish themselves in the narrative as a non-answer to a dubious need! And from their number comes the serpent. The effect of its activity is that the sharp juxtaposition of two views of the woman is blunted. Distance is put between her and ultimate responsibility for the fall (and, of course, the man is distanced from it further still). It may further be hazarded that the suggestion of *non-human* responsibility is important, as a distraction from the unavoidability of ascribing the *original* responsibility to Yahweh himself (§2.242; in the conceptual systems of later times the serpent will, of course, attract much speculation about its relation to Satan). All this the serpent theme achieves without resulting negativity to animals in general—the serpent bears the whole brunt of human resentment (3.15).

2.226 This discussion is related to what we have previously noted about the woman as a mediating category between the man and the animals (§2.122). She fluctuates between greater closeness to the man, which increases, for the purpose of the 'middle' semantics, the semblance of human unity, and greater closeness to the animals, which stresses that she and they together belong to the semantics of 'after'. This tension is particularly well illustrated by the theme of *naming*. In 2.19-20, the man names the animals. In 2.23 he names the woman, but in a strikingly different way. Not only is a different formula used but, more importantly, the man must *name himself* in order to name her—stressing mutuality in the 'middle' semantics.[11] In a sense, he does not name her at all, for the name he gives her, *'šh*, has been used of her already in the narrative (2.22), and he *renames himself* in conformity to it (*'yš* for *'dm*). However, in the 'after' situation of 3.20, he names the woman again; this time in the same way that he named the animals (cf. the formula), and with a name which associates her closely with the animals.

2.23   Life and knowledge: the two trees

2.231   It is, no doubt, in relation to *the isotopy of knowledge* that we see most clearly the instability of the logic of 'before'. The man's ignorance is hard to maintain narratively. Perhaps the most irreducible mystery is, Why did Yahweh put the tree of knowledge in the garden in the first place? From the very beginning, an element of 'after' existed 'before'. But we may pursue the theme of knowledge in other ways. Not only is the tree of knowledge present, but Yahweh must give the man *knowledge* of what the consequence will be if he eats of it (2.17), knowledge, that is, of the conditions of his existence! 2.18-25 is also most instructive. When elements of the 'after' configuration are presented to the man, in the form of the animals and the woman, he becomes, as it were, spontaneously knowledgeable. He *knows* he should name the animals, and how to; he *knows* that the woman is his counterpart, and defines himself in recognizing her (Naidoff: 6). Yahweh withdraws from the scene after introducing the new creatures into the man's world; the man, we sense, is in his own element (cf. Trible: 93).

2.232   Knowledge, then, is very much present in ch. 2, but covertly. It is only with the arrival of the serpent that the theme becomes overt, but even here it remains, necessarily, unexplained. How did the serpent come to be 'more subtle than any other animal' (3.1)? There is no answer; simply, the serpent is the *one who knows* what is going on, at least up to a point. But what is it which, according to the text, the serpent knows? It knows about knowledge, the conditions of knowledge. It knows that 'God knows', and it knows that *what* God knows is that the humans will also 'know', if they eat the fruit (3.5)! It knows that Yahweh is withholding knowledge that he has; even Yahweh's own knowledge is not withheld from the serpent. One recalls that the gnostics often made the serpent the hero of this story, not merely because it knows, but because it typifies what Hans Jonas has pointed out to be the characteristically gnostic knowledge—knowledge which is its own object. What the gnostics 'know' is that knowledge is salvation.[12] The figure of the serpent does indeed appear to correspond to this gnostic knowledge. Its point of view is that knowledge is salvation—i.e. *that one can know and remain in the garden.* But this proves to be false knowledge—the serpent by knowledge has deceived itself, as well as deceiving the humans. The knowledge that intrudes unexplained into the semantics of 'before' reveals itself as cunning opinion, unreliable. To gain knowledge is to gain the possibility of being in error!

2.233   *The isotopy of vitality* is less significant in connection with the 'middle' semantics. It is consistent with what has been said that death enters the 'before' situation as a possibility raised by the prohibition (2.17). It is perhaps worth mentioning also the serpent's well-known association in folklore with eternal, or infinitely renewable, life. In its double association, with knowledge (cunning) and with immortality, it seems to *embody* that compatibility between 'before' and 'after' which it affirms (cf. the previous paragraph). But the text makes clear that this is a delusion; the curse on the serpent (3.14) refers pointedly to its mortality ('all the days of your life').

2.234   One further point may be added about the two trees, a point which, even if partly 'spoken in jest' may yet be a 'true word'. Which tree is in the middle of the garden? 2.9 as it now reads is quite specific—it is the tree of life. 2.17 does not contradict this—the tree of knowledge is forbidden to the man, but it is not said to be in the middle of the garden. It is with 3.3 that the problem arises; the woman reports the divine prohibition in the form 'You shall not eat of the tree which is in the middle of the garden', referring, as the sequel shows, to the tree of knowledge. The narrative inconsistency can be 'explained', no doubt, in terms of the history of our text.[13] But, as is so frequently the case, narrative inconsistency creates startling semantic consistency (Güttgemanns: 49). 'Before', the tree of life was central—immortality belonged to that configuration, while knowledge did not! But in the 'middle' semantics, knowledge displaces immortality from the centre; obviously knowledge is for the woman the 'central' issue. Assuming that the man correctly reported to her a prohibition heard by him alone (2.17), perhaps she is guilty of the very first Freudian slip!

2.241   To summarize the mythic work, the myth has evoked a series of basic oppositions, to establish the seriousness of the fall, and partially broken them, in order to give a plausible account of the fall—how the system of 'before' *could* turn into that of 'after'. Yet the mythic work has been able to make a virtue of necessity—the forced creation of a 'middle' semantics has been turned to advantage by the agricultural, patriarchal mindset which generated the myth. This has occurred in two ways. First, it has been possible to idealize certain *limited* aspects of experience, even though they logically do not belong to the ideal of 'before'. Above all, an ideal dimension of the relationship between the sexes has been posited—though the myth sees sexual differentiation as causing much complexity and pain, it affirms within it an aspect of mutual joy. A basically innocent dimension of the human relationship with animals is similarly affirmed.

2.242   Secondly, and more importantly, the myth has achieved a desirable shift of guilt. Fall implies fault; that the man's existence was transformed from the ideal that God prepared for him implies an agent of this transformation. To press very far the idea of God's responsibility for evil is intolerable, but to accept all the guilt as the man's—that is, in the male mindset, as one's own—is no less intolerable. To create a bearable view of the world, some other candidates are needed. By means of the mythic work, the animals and the woman become available to share, or even assume, the guilt. The woman's presence in the garden, of course, makes the fall of the man into the fall of *humanity*—but not undifferentiatedly so. The woman was more guilty, eating the fruit first, instigating the man to do so; and she fell further, into that subordination which the patriarchal mindset roundly approves. But, beyond this, some of the weight can be removed from humanity altogether, and put on the mysterious non-human world, without being crassly loaded onto God. The animals are simply made available for this role, in a most arbitrary way, by the work of the myth. We have, in all, a magnificent obfuscation of the guilt for the fall: a bit of sexism, a bit of speculation about God and evil, a bit of resignation to evil as a mystery, and even a bit of acceptance of one's own guilt. Perhaps no one will notice that nothing has been explained. There is, though, a price to pay—the sense of the passivity of the man in the working out of his fate; to distance oneself from guilt is to admit one's limited power to affect things.

2.3 *Folk-tale* versus *myth*

2.31 The whole foregoing section (2.2) assumed the narrative model of the fall, the model of a myth of transformation. This, we saw earlier, corresponds to the dominant theme of the narrative; but it was a different narrative model, corresponding to a subordinate theme, which was better capable of unifying the text, namely the model of 'a man to till the earth'. The meaning of the text, as we have built it up through our investigation of the mythic work, is profoundly altered if one looks at the text in terms of this alternative model. In the fall model, the action is essentially mythic, that is, from the perspective of the community of the myth, *inevitable*; whatever is said about cause and fault (and we have seen that the myth works hard at this issue) the *outcome* is given and irreversible (cf. Kovacs: 145-46). The divine will is *single* and unalterable, and it is human fate to have become other than what God wills. The story of 'a man to till the earth' shows, on the other hand, a God *divided*, between a limited, simplified creation and an unlimited, complicated one. It shows 'all living' striving for unboundedness and complexity, and God finally cooperating in this—partly leading, partly led.[14] There was no 'fall'; the transformation from 'inside' to 'outside' was a gain, but was also a reestablishment of the norm.

2.32 This contrast between two views of our text can best be assessed in relation to the theme of knowledge, specifically the self-knowledge of the culture whose mindset generates the text. In the fall model, knowledge, the knowledge the myth conveys, is, in a sense, itself the fall. To *know oneself* fallen and to *be* fallen are the same thing, in as much as unfallenness was ignorance. Fallenness knows itself as such—it is essential to the definition of fallenness that we can posit the unfallenness from which we are excluded. Now, as we have seen, unfallenness cannot be posited in any self-consistent way, though the text strives hard to do so. Within the mythic universe, the unreal is valued above the real, and immense effort is expended to preserve the reality of the unreal! In the perspective of 'a man to till the earth', the real is valued, through hard struggle, above the unreal. Rather than beckoning us away from a reality from which we cannot, in fact, escape, the unreal functions to instruct us about reality; our ultimate inability to define the unreal as real obliges us and teaches us to value the world we know. Our text, we may say, works as a means of sorting out experience and dream, living with both, but opting for experience.

2.33 'The tension at work in this narrative seems to reflect a basic inability to decide whether man's terrestrial environment, intellect, labor and sexuality are to be assessed positively or negatively' (Casalis: 47). Casalis has well observed the tension, but I do not believe he is correct to see the text as a balanced statement of two possibilities considered at the same level (he goes on to speak of a 'final redactor' who 'took into account opposite views'). Rather, we have a dominant narrative, that of the fall, presented in a way whch creates deep problems and an alternative, 'recessive' narrative which undermines but fails to replace the dominant one.[15]

2.34 Superficially, dream has won out. Our text has characteristically been regarded as 'the fall'. In the main tradition of interpretation, God remains one and authoritative; the incoherence of the character Yahweh has been concealed for the most part successfully. 'Man' remains with his fate and his fault, yet with the compensation of being able to blame the world more than he blames himself, to see himself as a partially innocent victim, to feel that 'his' God has made things even worse for those who instigated his fault; and with the security of a sure and simplistic vision of how things *ought* to be. Yet it seems that this view of our text does not deeply satisfy, for the text continues to attract to itself an immense *discourse of interpretation*. Is not this discourse the continuation of the mythic work, consisting, as mythic work characteristically does, of *talking around* our deepest cultural contradictions (Vol. I/1 §3.2).

3. *Implications for feminist exegesis*

3.0 As might be expected in view of the dominantly patriarchal tradition of exegesis of Gen. 2.4b–3.24, one recent focus of this discourse of interpretation has been in feminist scholarship. The fullest and best-known feminist exegesis has been that of Trible (1978). Deeply as I am in sympathy with her larger aims, it will be clear from my foregoing treatment how wholly out of sympathy I am with Trible's approach to this particular text. The issues between us seem to me of sufficient importance and generality to merit discussion.

3.11   Our text is for Trible the account of a tragedy. She works within the conceptuality of the fall, but a fall which is unambiguously that of humanity as a whole, both sexes together. Lack of equality and mutuality between the sexes is entirely a *result* of the fall, indeed one of its major results. The male has no priority over the female in creation, nor does she take priority over him in disobedience. In summary, the story of the fall of humanity is told in Genesis without any interruption of sexism into what the text perceives as the divinely willed order of things.

3.12   Several specific aspects of Trible's exegesis need to be challenged. First, she interprets the *'dm*, the human actor at the beginning of the text, as a sexually undifferentiated 'earth-creature' (Trible: 80; page references hereafter are to Trible). Sexual differentiation comes only with the creation of the woman, a view borne out by the use of *'yš*, man as opposed to woman, for the first time in 2.23 (97-98). But it is surely clear that the primal human is perceived as male. The word *'dm* which is used for this creature continues to be used in the later part of the text for the man as opposed to the woman (indeed, as soon as 2.25); this Trible admits, but fails to explain it satisfactorily (98). The agricultural work of the *'dm* (2.15) is specifically *male* work in 3.17-19. The body from which the woman is taken is surely perceived as male (the alternative is that it became male during the operation!). The logic of the issue is, of course, all on Trible's side. Maleness is meaningless before sexual differentiation. The originality of maleness over femaleness is affirmed in the text against logic, but it is affirmed.

3.13   Secondly, Trible insists on the absolute equality of the woman's and the man's offences (3.6) in eating the fruit (112-14). Each is fully responsible for her or his action. This, of course, is true in itself, but it takes no account of the asymmetry of the offences. The woman sinned first, and was implicated in the man's sin; the man did not sin first, nor was he implicated in the woman's sin. Why should the text be saying nothing significant through this clear asymmetry when—especially for a skilled rhetorical critic like Trible—much smaller details have large significance? Instigation to sin is viewed extremely negatively in many parts of the Bible (e.g. 1 Kgs 15.26 and its many parallels; Matt. 18.7; cf. also §2.223).

3.14   One might pursue other details of exegesis; or, at a more general level, one might explore how locked Trible is into seeing the fall of humanity as the full scope of our text (she is very unwilling to take up the mystery of evil, the significance of the serpent, etc.; see 111). But the question which must surely be addressed to her the most urgently is: Who, in a patriarchal culture, composed the feminist story which she takes the text to be; and how was it received, by a patriarchal culture, as its basic myth of origins? It is a 'man's world' which tells the biblical stories, even the stories of women; this is precisely the point of view Trible herself adopts in dealing with Ruth elsewhere in the same book (166-99; note the first sentence on p. 166), and which she develops superbly. Why does she not apply the same principle to Gen 2.4b–3.24? Of this, as of any other biblical text—but most particularly of those which present women and female experience most positively—it must be asked, why is it acceptable to patriarchal assumptions, indeed how does it subserve these assumptions?

3.21   In several ways, and at several levels, my treatment of Gen. 2.4b–3.24 shows a more or less positive attitude towards woman functioning in the text. The introduction of the serpent as tempter softens the theme of the woman's special responsibility for the fall—one can conceive of a much *more* sexist text. 2.23-25 suggests that, at some level of consciousness, the dream of an equal relationship between the sexes operates (though, at least in vv. 23 and 24a, it is still equality expressed from a male perspective). Perhaps more striking still is that, at the critical moment of the fall, the woman appears as active and intelligent, the man as passive and unaware (so Trible: 113). But it is just here, surely, that one is obliged to ask how such characterizations come to be in a patriarchal text. I have suggested that they are inevitable expressions of the logic of the myth: woman and sexuality belong to the same semantic configuration as knowledge. Part of the price the male mindset pays is the admission that woman is more aware of the complexity of the world, more in touch with 'all living'. And finally, at the deepest level of the text, where the fall myth as a whole is in tension with 'a man to till the earth', the possibility is evoked that the human transformation in which the woman took powerful initiative was positive, rather than negative, that the complex human world is to be preferred over any male ideal.

3.22   But these 'positive' features are not the direct expression of a feminist consciousness (or even a consciousness *more* feminist, for some reason, that is usual in the Bible). Rather, they are the effects of the patriarchal mindset tying itself in knots trying to account for woman and femaleness in a way which *both* makes sense *and* supports patriarchal assumptions. Given that there must be *two* sexes, why cannot they be *really one* (2.23-25)? Why must woman be different and act *independently* (which surely is her real fault in 3.1-6)? In the face of the irreducible twoness, the text strives for a false unity by making maleness the norm, and accounting for human experience by making 'humanity as male' its protagonist; but it fails in this, for 'humanity as male and female' inevitably reasserts itself as the true protagonist.

3.23   Feminist exegetes have, to my knowledge, showed little interest in structural methods.[16] But surely there is a profound connection between such methods and feminist hermeneutics. At one level, the aim of the feminist programme is to show that how things now appear does not correspond to the nature of things—that the surface structures of the world are out of alignment with the deep structures! If this be so, then feminist theology is not forced to choose between *rejection* of the Bible as wholly patriarchal and *denial* that the Bible *is* wholly patriarchal. The third option is to accept the Bible as everywhere patriarchal, but as everywhere expressive, for that very reason, of the bad conscience that goes along with trying to make sense of patriarchalism; and conceptually vulnerable, therefore, to the kind of deconstructive literary approach which I have adopted here (cf. Introduction §4).

Chapter 2

DEUTERONOMIC POLITICAL THEORY
IN JUDGES AND 1 SAMUEL 1–12

The Book of Samuel has been called the Biblical *Politeia*. The
Book of Judges deserves the same designation (Buber: 84).

. . . we had first of all to agree that all the myths are *saying
something*; and then to verify that the Wabanaki myths are not just
saying something other than the Loon Woman myths . . .: they are
contradicting them . . . (Lévi-Strauss, 1981: 209).

0.   *Introduction*

0.1   This analysis is a companion piece to 'Jonathan' (Vol. I/1). In
the introduction to that study, I explained its relationship to the work
of D.J. McCarthy (1973) on 1 Sam. 8–12. He read these five
chapters, in all their traditio-historical diversity, as a unified whole,
whose achievement is the incorporation of monarchy into Israel's
theological system—an impressive achievement, because Israel's
theology is resistant to monarchy. He set out to show·how the
arrangement of the parts of 1 Sam. 8–12 permits statement of the
opposed points of view regarding monarchy, and their satisfactory
reconciliation. In 'Jonathan', I looked at the following chapters (1
Sam. 13–31) from a related point of view—what is the theological
problem which is getting worked on in this narrative? I concluded
that it is the problem of explaining how kingship could be 'lawfully'
transferred from Saul's house to David, given that the dynastic
principle is intrinsic to kingship.

0.21   Here, I shall move in the opposite direction, backwards from 1
Sam. 8–12. For this section is only the culmination of a long

sequence in the Deuteronomic History. This history is organized by means of programmatic theological passages (McCarthy, 1965: 131, following Noth: 5-6). One such passage is Judg. 2.6–3.6, which includes the theory of judgeship (§1.111), and the next is 1 Sam. 12, the formal passage from judgeship to kingship (§1.13). The whole section Judg. 2.11 (I choose this as the beginning since it is where the 'theory' of the judge-period begins) through 1 Sam. 12 broaches the question, 'What form of government is appropriate for Israel?'

0.22   The specific terms in this 'debate' are, of course, judgeship and monarchy. In Judg. 2.11–16.31, judgeship takes centre-stage (though monarchy is anticipated, chs. 6–9), and in 1 Sam. 8–12, monarchy comes to the fore (though judgeship continues to be considered, especially in ch. 12). How should we characterize the intervening material? Formally, as I shall show, it has been incorporated into the judge-period (§1.12).[1] Materially, Judg. 17–21 says nothing of judgeship, but it contributes to the 'debate' in looking forward specifically to monarchy (17.6, 21.25, etc.). 1 Sam. 1-7, on the other hand, says virtually nothing of monarchy (2.10 and 35 allude to it), but brings judgeship back into the debate (4.18; ch. 7).[2]

0.31   Virtually all interpreters identify pro- and anti-monarchical parts of our text, and the recent trend is to treat the tension redaction-critically. Typical is Veijola (52 and *passim*), who identifies an earlier and pro-monarchical (DtrG) and a later and anti-monarchical (DtrN) version of the Deuteronomic History [3]. But such treatments cannot avoid the problem of why the final form of the text brings together such apparently opposed points of view. Buber, who sees Judges as the editorial combination of preexisting pro- and anti-monarchical books (e.g. 68), poses the question well: 'But how could two literary works, produced by such opposing purposes, be joined to one another without nullifying not only the unity but also the credibility of the resulting book . . . ?' (83).

0.32   What, in other words, is the final form of the Deuteronomic History *doing*? The work seems to me to become simply unreadable as a literary text when an interpreter like Crüsemann (e.g. 15, 45-46) is content to regard it as little more than a juxtaposition of points of view of various age and provenance, for the combination of which no one, as it were, takes responsibility. Veijola presumably sees his DtrN as taking responsibility; but he nowhere explains why this anti-monarchical editor let stand the opposed point of view. Buber (83) is more satisfactory; he speaks of a deliberate editorial 'balancing' of points of view, and in this he is close to McCarthy's view of 1 Sam. 8–12 as a successful resolution of the theological issue of monarchy.

0.33   The deuteronomic editors, in their post-exilic situation, were no doubt occupied with the question: What do the old traditions about monarchy mean now that the monarchy is no more? Perhaps they were in a situation where the question of government in Israel was a genuinely open one, where monarchy was a real possibility (one thinks of the time of Zerubbabel)—on this, one can do little more than speculate. But at least we can say that the history is a coming to terms with Israel's pro- and anti-monarchical traditions for some such situation in life. Buber has the post-exilic situation in mind as he attempts to define the 'message' of the final form of Judges: 'Out of the book, thus understood, [post-Exilic Judaism] could draw instruction and admonition' (84).[4]

0.34   But a 'balancing' or a 'successful resolution' of such a profound contradiction as exists in Israel's view of monarchy did not and could not, in my view, occur. I prefer it when Buber speaks of 'two antithetical parts (being) true simultaneously', and especially when he asserts that the final form 'had to succeed and did succeed' (83). These statements are suggestive of Lévi-Strauss's view of contradiction in myth, which I follow here just as I did in 'Jonathan' (Vol. I/1 §3.21). If the Deuteronomic History does not present a clear 'point of view' towards monarchy, may this not be because its editors do not have one? I speculate that if I could ask them whether, in their view, the restoration of the monarchy would be a good thing, I would get a complicated rather than a simple answer! My analysis will, I believe, demonstrate that the deuteronomic treatment of monarchy is a classic example of talking around a contradiction.[5] This does not mean that the editors say nothing intelligible about monarchy, but rather that what they say is very complex. We are not in a position to say to what extent this complexity expresses an 'intentional' message. They let stand a very basic contradiction in Israel's system, perhaps because they perceived, or sensed, that it was a contradiction that Israel should go on living *within*. These editors, whatever their intention, took responsibility for their complex statement, and no doubt wished by it to provide Buber's 'instruction and admonition' in their generation.[6] Those who canonized the text took responsibility for its complexity. And, in our day, so do we critics.

0.4   In Part 1, I shall consider the whole section Judg. 2.11–1 Sam. 12 as a debate between judgeship and kingship. I shall then, in Part 2, move to a text within the text, Judg. 6–9 (Gideon and Abimelech), which is a lengthy proleptic consideration of monarchy. In the conclusion (Part 3) I shall summarize first how Judg. 6–9 informs the reading of 1 Sam. 8–12, and then how Judg. 2.11–1 Sam. 12 as a whole functions in the creation of the Deuteronomists' theology of government.

1.   *Government in the larger text: Judges 2.11–1 Samuel 12*

1.1   The cyclical pattern of the judges

1.11   The establishment of the pattern in Judg. 2.11–16.31

1.111 The period of rule by 'judges' in Israel is inaugurated by a programmatic passage, Judg. 2.11-19, which summarizes the period as a series of repetitions of the following cyclical scheme:

1.   Israel falls into apostasy against Yahweh.
2.   A foreign oppressor dominates Israel for a time.
3.   Israel appeals to Yahweh.[7]
4.   Yahweh attends the appeal, and sends a judge to save Israel.
5.   The judge defeats the oppressor.
6.   Israel remains faithful to Yahweh during the judge's lifetime, and suffers no external threat.

After the judge's death, renewed apostasy begins a new cycle. While Judg. 2.11-19 does not express all of this with perfect clarity,[8] almost all dubious points in it are resolved by the first cycle, that of Othniel (3.7-11), which seems designed to exemplify the entire cycle with utmost brevity. In my analysis, I shall take points 3 to 6 as constituting the 'judge-cycle' proper, and points 1 and 2 the 'gap' between cycles. I include point 3 in the cycle since it immediately precipitates the judge's rise.

1.112   Despite many vicissitudes, to be considered, this cycle is evident, through six repetitions, as far as Judg. 16. The following are the six judges (often referred to as 'major judges') for whom the pattern is manifested (the missing sections are the gaps):

Othniel	Judg. 3.9-11
Ehud	Judg. 3.15-30
Deborah	Judg. 4.3–5
Gideon	Judg. 6.7–8.32
Jephthah	Judg. 10.10–12.7
Samson	Judg. 13.2–16

1.1130   The cyclical pattern does not, however, proceed predictably. In particular, various non-standard things happen in the gaps, of which the following are relevant to my analysis.

1.1131   *The 'minor judges'*. This is a term traditionally applied to Shamgar (Judg. 3.31), Tola and Jair (10.1-5), and Ibzan, Elon, and Abdon (12.8-15). The notices of these are similar in most formal features (Shamgar is the most divergent[9]); in particular, each notice begins with 'after him', implying that each directly followed another judge, either major or minor (in 10.1, the formula is 'after Abimelech'; whether or not he was any kind of a judge, Tola followed him directly).

1.1132   *Development of a 'gap': Gideon and Abimelech*. Aside from the interruptions of the 'minor judges', the gaps between Othniel, Ehud, Deborah, and Gideon, and again between Jephthah and Samson, are dealt with routinely—Israel sins and falls under foreign domination, in accordance with the pattern. But the gap between the Gideon and Jephthah cycles (Judg. 8.33–9.57) is extended and not routine. At 8.33 a new cycle seems to begin (the wording is normal for point 1), but no foreign oppressor appears, and this cycle goes no further. Formally, the whole Abimelech section ought then to be a description of the apostasy into which Israel fell after the death of Gideon. I do not mean that the Abimelech traditions developed in connection with the cyclical pattern, but rather that, since the pattern creates the gaps *programmatically*, there is *room* for traditions to be incorporated to indicate what the gaps were like, and hence, perhaps, what they *mean*.

1.1133   *The compounding of judge-cycles: Jephthah and Samson*. Othniel, Ehud, Deborah, and Gideon face each a clearly identified oppressor, and defeat it utterly—that is, each fully solves the given problem. With Jephthah, something quite new and startling occurs. There are *two* oppressors, Philistines and Ammonites (10.7), and, though Jephthah deals comprehensively with the Ammonites, there is no mention at all of his doing anything about the Philistines. Correspondingly, the Philistines persist as the oppressor in the next cycle (13.1; Webb: 234). Nor does even Samson fully overcome them (the characteristic subjugation formula is missing).[10]

1.12 The extension of the pattern in Judg. 17–1 Sam. 7

1.120 Where is the narrative to go after Samson? It cannot remain locked for ever in a series of major judge-cycles. And we expect the unfinished business of the Philistine threat to be resolved.

1.1211 In fact, we find in 1 Samuel evidence of the resumption of the system of major judge-cycles. For Eli, the evidence is confined to 4.18, 'He had judged Israel forty years'. While this formula is most characteristic of the 'minor judges' (but cf. Judg. 16.31), the length of time is characteristic of the major cycles (Judg. 3.11, 30, 5.31). Only in this quite formal sense is Eli one of the judges. His 'judgeship' is in every way irregular; least of all is it a time of faithfulness to Yahweh. But this makes 1 Sam. 4.18 all the more interesting; the fiction of the text is that the judge-cycles continued after Samson.

1.1212 At this formal level, Judg. 17–21 functions as the gap between Samson and Eli. It was a time of apostasy—though the text does not employ the usual formula of 'going after the Baals and the Ashtaroth', it does stress cultic irregularity within Yahweh-worship (chs. 17–18; cf. Boling: 254-67, Soggin: 268, 277). Apostasy leads to distress, which takes the form of *internecine strife* (§1.25) rather than foreign oppression (the Philistine oppression, though it has never formally come to an end, is not mentioned in these chapters). The nearest approach to a 'cry to Yahweh' (21.3) is in connection with the internecine strife. Most importantly, the bad conditions of this period are repeatedly explained as due to the want of a 'king in Israel' (17.6; 21.25; cf. 18.1; 19.1).

1.122 1 Sam. 4.19–7.17 exhibits a remarkable logical conformity to the standard cycle, and sufficient formal conformity to suggest that

Samuel is being put forward intentionally as one of the judges (according to the six-point scheme introduced above, §1.111):

1. The 'gap', which consists of 4.19–7.2, is not presented directly in terms of apostasy. But Samuel later implies that it has been precisely a time of apostasy, and Israel accepts the charge (7.3-6; note the parallels to Judg. 3.7, 10.10, etc.)

2. This period was one of foreign domination. A length of time— 'twenty years'—is given (1 Sam. 7.2; cf. Judg. 3.8, etc.). This refers to the absence of the ark, but that very absence is a metonym for foreign oppression.

3. Israel's appeal to Yahweh in 1 Sam. 7.6 comes, anomalously, *after* the appearance of the judge-deliverer, and at his instigation. In the regular cycle, the judge appears following the appeal. But the end of 7.2, though it is obscure,[11] perhaps implies repentance and appeal to Yahweh even before Samuel's (re-)appearance—certainly Samuel himself suggests this possibility in v. 3.

4. The appearance of Samuel at 7.3 is odd. His career began earlier, and reached a culmination in 3.19–4.1, where he appeared established as a leader in Israel. But since then he has been completely absent. It is fair to say that it is in 7.3 that he first appears *in his judge role*. His earlier career suggests again a concern for *continuity*; there is something like a formal succession from Eli to Samuel (§1.2122).

5. Samuel's defeat of the Philistine oppressor could not be clearer (7.3, 7-11, 13-14). Note especially the formula that the Philistines were 'subdued' (7.13; cf. Judg. 3.30, 11.33, etc.)

6. The subjugation of the Philistines persists 'all the days of Samuel' (1 Sam. 7.13), and there is internal peace too (7.14). 'Samuel judged Israel all the days of his life' (7.15), suggesting that he maintained Israel's faithful relationship to Yahweh.

1.123   We have evidence, therefore, for the artificial resumption of the major judge-cycles in 1 Samuel; specifically, the following new cycles are defined:

Eli:	1 Sam. 1.1–4.18
Samuel:	1 Sam. 7.3-17

In defining these new cycles, we define also two new 'gaps'—Judg. 17–21 and 1 Sam. 4.19–7.2. Formally, we have an answer to our earlier question—what happens after Samson? The major judge-cycles continue for a time. And the Philistine threat, left as unfinished business at the end of the Samson-cycle, is resolved in the clearest terms by Samuel (1 Sam. 7.13).[12]

1.13   1 Sam. 8–12 and the judge-pattern

1.131   Even more pressingly than after Samson, the question now must be, what comes next? What ought to follow, in the logic of the judge-cycle, is Samuel's death. Instead, he installs his sons as judges (8.1-3), a move not compatible with the theory, and the failure of which leads to the establishment of a different system of government, monarchy. The period of the judges has apparently given way to that of the kings, in agreement with the general biblical picture (cf. note 1).

1.132   But there is a little more to be said. In the structure of the Deuteronomic History, the formal transition from the judges to the kings comes not after 1 Sam. 7, but only with Samuel's valedictory speech in ch. 12 (§0.21). The period of the judges lives on in Samuel,[13] creating an uncomfortable overlap with the beginning of monarchy. The content of the speech confirms the point, for in it Samuel vindicates not only himself but also the system he represents. This is especially clear in 12.9-11, where the adequacy and appropriateness of the judge-system is affirmed with unequalled clarity. These three verses include the whole theory of the standard judge-cycle in exactly the terms of Judg. 2.11-19. None of the problems and complexities of the actual experience of judgeship in the long intervening chapters receive any notice here. Judgeship is right and adequate and *should not be giving way to monarchy.*

1.133   In 1 Sam. 8–12, then, the text is so arranged as to view the rise of monarchy within the logic which the judge-cycles established, and to invite comparison between the two systems of government. In fact, though the judge-cycles are over, there are features in the text reminiscent of them, as though a new, paradoxical cycle were beginning (§1.361): In 8.8, the language used ('forsaking me and serving other gods') is very like the apostasy formulae in point 1 of the cycle; and ch. 11 follows the pattern of foreign oppression and the raising of a deliverer (points 2 and 4).

1.2   Isotopic analysis

1.20   In this section, I shall consider in turn certain large themes related to leadership, and work out the logic of each in our text (for the terminology, Introduction §5.2). I shall begin with what seems clearly the dominant isotopy, that of *continuity vs. discontinuity* of leadership, and with certain matters directly related to continuity, in particular *hereditary* rule; then I shall take up in order *divine vs. human initiative* in the choice of rulers, *quality of leadership*, above all the ruler's effect on Israel's relationship to Yahweh, *foreign oppression*, and *internecine strife*. On all of these, with the possible exception of the last, the logic of the judge-cycle itself implies a point of view; we shall therefore take particular interest in failures of the text to conform to this point of view. Each isotopy will help fill out the structure of the kingship *vs.* judgeship debate.

1.21   Continuity of government

1.2111   As a system of leadership, the judge-system has built-in hiatuses; after each judge there is neither a successor *nor a procedure for getting one.* The long sequence of events through which a new judge will eventually appear must be set in motion by Israel's renewed apostasy. *Continuity/discontinuity of rulership* are the terms of a code thus established as important for the judge-period. I previously identified three ways in which the standard judge-cycle is modified (§1.113), and each of these seems to me to represent a textual counteraction in the direction of *continuity*, in the face of the problems raised by the discontinuity of the cyclical pattern. I am not here concerned, of course, with the possible history of various offices in Israel, but with textual effects.

1.2112   First, the minor judges embody a system of *continuous* government, quite at odds with the cyclical pattern.[14] The concern for continuity is underlined by the facts (a) that the sequences of minor judges get longer (one alone, two together, three together), and (b) that one of the major judges, Jephthah, has been integrated into a minor judge sequence (12.7).

1.2113   Second, the two sections which, as I have argued, offer explicit reflection on the 'gaps' in the judge-cycles, Judge. 8.33–9.57 and chs. 17–21, are exactly the two places where kingship, an intrinsically *continuous* form of government, is put forward as an alternative to judgeship.

1.2114 Third, the compounding of the judge-cycles may be interpreted as another kind of pressure towards continuity. The same enemy, the Philistines, remains undefeated through the cycles of Jephthah, Samson, and Eli, and is overcome only by Samuel. The nature of foreign oppression fails to conform to the one-by-one treatment of foreign oppressors in the standard cycle.

1.2121 The concern for continuity can be traced in other ways; perhaps in the theme of the call of the judge (Samson, Samuel) *from birth*, and certainly in the succession from Eli to Samuel. But much the most important of these aspects of continuity is *heredity*. It first appears as a theme in the Gideon-cycle, where the possibility is raised that a son of Gideon may succeed him (Judg. 8.22), a possibility which then dominates the text through ch. 9. But the sons or children of judges remain a theme after Abimelech. The text informs us about the sons and sometimes the daughters of several minor judges (Jair, Ibzan, Abdon), for no apparent reason (but cf. §2.3441). Jephthah's childlessness is central to the account of his judgeship.[15]

1.2122 In the cases of Eli and Samuel, the continuance of the judge's office (even in his lifetime) by his sons, is envisaged. All these sons are faithless and unworthy (1 Sam. 2.12-17, 22-25, etc.; 8.1-3, 5). The two cases, of Eli and of Samuel, are, though, asymmetrical. Eli is nowhere presented very positively, and the failings of his sons are laid expressly at his door (1 Sam. 2.29; 3.13). The sins of Eli's sons lead to the rise of Samuel as a surrogate 'son' (3.6, 16) and successor to Eli (this I take to be the significance of his early career in 1 Sam. 3.1–4.1, before the beginning of his judge-cycle). Samuel's leadership, on the other hand, is presented positively; but this makes it only the more striking that his sons are no better than Eli's. In the framework of the judge-cycles, *any* tendency towards hereditary leadership has negative results; every son of a judge who achieves a leadership role (Abimelech; Hophni and Phinehas; Joel and Abijah) exercises it badly.

1.2131 The rise of monarchy in 1 Sam. 8–12 is obviously a move to

continuous and hereditary government. The people's request for a
king is set in the context of a concern for *continuity* of leadership:
'Behold, you [Samuel] are old and your sons do not walk in your
ways' (8.5). The elders perhaps recall bitter experience of what
happens after the death of a judge. The outcome of their request is a
new system which meets their concern. Yet the treatment of continuity
and heredity in these chapters is paradoxical, and in two ways.

1.2132   First, the initiative which leads to monarchy is Samuel's
own; it is his attempt to establish his sons as judges which provokes
the people's request for a king. I shall later deal more fully with the
key role of 8.1-3 in achieving the transition from judgeship to
kingship (§1.334). Suffice it to say here that it is *just* when Samuel
has gloriously reestablished the integrity of judgeship (ch. 7) that he
tries to subvert its very nature, into a continuous, hereditary system;
and thereby precipitates the replacement of judgeship by a continuous,
hereditary system. Kingship is born of a concern for continuity felt
by the last of the judges![16]

1.2133   Second, it is most striking that in 1 Sam. 8.4–12.25 there is no
mention at all of kingship as hereditary, of any succession to King
Saul. The respect in which kingship most plainly stands over against
judgeship, its continuity, is not made an issue. It might be argued
that this omission was due to an awareness that Saul would not, in
fact, found a dynasty; but the text assumes kingship to be dynastic, as
13.13-14 already shows.[17] Some other explanation is needed for the
apparent reticence at this point to stress heredity as part of the *theory*
of kingship.

1.22   Initiative in the establishment of leaders

1.221   Israel's judges, according to the cyclical pattern, are to be
chosen by Yahweh, and the isotopy of initiative in establishing Israel's
leadership is a very important one. Divine initiative is clearly present
in most of the eight judge-cycles. It is most conspicuously absent in
the case of Eli, who, as we have seen, is the most divergent of all the
judges from the norm. It is not made specific in the case of Deborah,
who is made to appear as a judge-in-place, like one of the minor
judges (Judg. 4.4-5); but there is no reason to doubt a general
initiative of Yahweh here. The most striking exception to the pattern

of divine initiative in the rise of the major judges is Jephthah—humans carry the story forward in Judg. 10.18–11.11. There is nothing of divine initiative in the rise of the minor judges, and Abimelech stands alone in the judge-period as a leader who rises in large measure *by his own initiative*. The pattern is reasonably clear; major judges are chosen by Yahweh, minor judges not. It is the discontinuous system which preserves divine initiative, whereas the continuous system disregards it. The exception of Jephthah from the pattern of divine initiative is odd (though Webb: 72-73, 85-89 aptly refers to Yahweh's closeness to Jephthah in 11.11, 29); but perhaps it is relevant to recall that he is the one among the major judges to be virtually incorporated (Judg. 12.7) among the minor ones. The irregularity of his rise may, in any case, be seen as one more marker of the gradual 'fall' from the ideal of the judge-cycles (§1.322).

1.222 The establishment of Saul is by the people's initiative but also by divine choice. The people desire a king, but they do not choose one for themselves; Yahweh does it, through the agency of Samuel. The stories of the secret anointing (9.1–10.16) and the public acceptance (10.17-25) of Saul stress divine initiative, notably in the use of the sacred lot. We may note also the theme of Saul's lowly origins (9.21; cf. 10.21) which recalls directly the Gideon-tradition in Judg. 6.15; Gideon's insignificance underscored the freedom of divine choice.[18] One of the theoretical problems of monarchy is the preservation of divine initiative when heredity is established. This problem does not arise in 1 Sam. 8–12, since in the first beginning of a monarchy divine choice can be affirmed.

1.23 Quality of leadership

1.231 Another, somewhat related, theme is the *quality* of leadership. The theory of the judge-cycle is that the judge is an exemplary leader life-long, able in particular to keep Israel faithful to Yahweh (Judg. 2.16-19). But, starting with Gideon, the issue begins to arise of the faithless judge, who tends even to lead Israel into faithlessness. Gideon not only goes astray but leads Israel astray (8.24-27). Thereafter, the same theme of the faithless judge remains in play in various ways. The status of Jephthah vis-à-vis Yahweh is obscure; but it is scarcely to his credit that he bargains with Yahweh over his forthcoming campaign, a bargain which gets Jephthah into religious jeopardy[19] and leads to family disaster (Judg. 11.30-31, 34-39). Samson fails to hold to his Nazirite vows, and the text suggests that his selfishness and incontinence thwart Yahweh's purposes. Eli does not lead Israel astray, but his sons do, and he gets some of the blame (1 Sam. 2.29; 3.13).

1.232   Samuel in ch. 7 is the model leader of Israel in faithfulness to Yahweh, and in chs. 8–12 (and beyond) he continues to deliver Yahweh's words and carry out Yahweh's behests; above all, in ch. 12, he vindicates himself and the system he has embodied over against the new system of kingship. But the contrast drawn between judgeship and monarchy is less strong than might be expected; relatively little is made in chs. 8–12 of the possibility that the *king* may lead the people into *unfaithfulness* to Yahweh. Samuel's critique of monarchy in 8.11-17 is scathing, but it does not take up the matter of leading the people astray (for example by cultic intrusions). Even in ch. 12 it is the people's own initiative for evil, rather than the king's leading them into it, which Samuel raises. (On the tendency of kings to lead their people astray, cf. Vol. I/3.) As to Saul, the text adopts a *nihil nisi bonum* attitude towards him through ch. 12; in particular he comes out on the right side in various scenes with cultic implications (10.10-13; 11.6-7, 13).

1.24   Foreign oppression

1.241   In 1 Sam. 8.20, the people request a king 'to go out before us and fight our battles'; and in the prevailing historicist tradition of scholarship, it is accepted that the rise of monarchy in Israel was the result of external military threat—if the judge-system worked reasonably well before the appearance of the Philistines, it was wholly inadequate to deal with the threat which they presented. There is no reason to doubt the historical accuracy of this view, but it is not the view of the text. Foreign oppression, in the logic of the judge-cycles, is entirely the consequence of unfaithfulness, and it is dealt with completely by the judge. As the discontinuous pattern tends towards continuity, indeed, so foreign oppression (the Philistines) tends towards continuity; but even this oppression is overcome when a faithful judge leads the people in faithfulness (1 Sam. 7; cf. §1.324).[20]

1.242   Seen in this light, the concern of the people in 1 Sam. 8.20

about foreign enemies comes at a time when they have and can have no such enemies; Samuel has fully dealt with the Philistines in ch. 7, and, within the logic of the judge-period, there will be peace at least for his lifetime (we may note that 7.14 makes this *pax iudicis* even more comprehensive, taking in also 'the Amorites'). The defence which Samuel makes of judgeship in ch. 12 reaffirms this logic; judgeship has shown itself perfectly adequate to deal with foreign oppression (vv. 10-11).

1.243   Yet this affirmation of Samuel and judgeship takes nothing away from Saul. He appears in 1 Sam. 8–12 as one who will *recapitulate* the work of the judges, of Samuel in particular, but go beyond it. He first defeats the Ammonites (ch. 11), the enemy which, we recall, was paired with the Philistines in the preamble to the Jephthah-cycle (Judg. 10.7); and he will go on to save Israel from the Philistines themselves (9.16; note the modelling of this verse on the judge-cycles, and cf. McCarthy, 1973: 411-12)—despite the fact that Samuel has already done so (7.14)! Beyond even this, Saul will save Israel 'from the hand of their enemies round about' (10.1, reading with LXX; cf. Veijola: 118). Unlike the judges, who dealt each with a single enemy, Saul is to provide *permanent* and *general* protection from all enemies.

1.25   Internecine conflict

1.251   This isotopy is inverse to that of foreign oppression. Unlike the leadership which precedes (Moses-Joshua, §1.3252) and follows (the united monarchy), judgeship (both major and minor) is related to tribalism—there is typically much attention to the judge's tribe. The question, therefore, arises, whether the system will *keep Israel together*. There is a portentous hint as early as Ehud of conflict between tribal identity and national unity—his attachment to Benjamin separates him from the main body of Israelites, whom he calls out *after* his individual exploit (Judg. 3.27-28). They respond, and all is well. But under the next leader, Deborah, not all the tribes respond (5.15-17), and even between her and Barak there is a sense of tribal tension (4.6-10). Gideon gets into conflict, barely resolved, with the Ephraimites, over his conduct of the Midianite war (7.24–8.3), and Jephthah even ends up at war with the Ephraimites (12.1-6). Internecine strife appears briefly in the Samson-cycle (15.9-13), but is absent from 1 Sam. 1–7.[21]

1.252   Internecine strife is a central feature of the 'gaps' in 8.33–9.57 and chs. 17–21. Abimelech's career begins with his setting of his mother's kin-group (Shechem) against that of Gideon, his father, and concludes in other intratribal squabbles (the one who aspires to rule 'over Israel', 9.22, cannot unify a tribe or even a city!). In ch. 18, the Danites come in conflict with the house of Micah. In chs. 19–21, above all, we find an ironic comment on the aspirations of judgeship to be able to unify Israel. The Levite, on no divine initiative, calls out the tribes not, as the judges do, to fight a foreign oppressor, but to discipline an enemy within. Chs. 17–21 perhaps portray an inchoate striving for unity (from individual to tribe, 17.19, from tribe to nation, especially 21.3) with no systemic base.

1.253   The gaps in the judge-period, then, leave Israel prey to anarchy; but even when Yahweh *does* raise up a judge, this provides no guarantee at all against internal strife; the problem, rather, increases from judge to judge.

1.254   There is very little of internal strife in the accounts of Saul's rise. His call to the tribes in ch. 11 receives unanimous support, in contrast to most of the calls to the tribes made by the judges, and his own tribal attachment never becomes divisive. But Samuel's anti-monarchical speech in 1 Sam. 8.11-18 foresees another kind of internal strife, between king and people, that is, *tyranny*. Saul himself conspicuously refuses to be a tyrant. He will not deal harshly with those who doubt his abilities (10.26-27; 11.12-13). The only possible model for royal tyranny in Israel, up to 1 Sam. 12, is Abimelech (cf. Part 2).

1.3   Summary of the analysis of Judg. 2.11–1 Sam. 12

1.31   Deut. 17: Permission for kingship

1.311   The debate about kingship in the Deuteronomic History is governed by the formulation of Deut. 17.14-17:

> 'When you come to the land which Yahweh your God gives you, and you possess it and dwell in it, and then say, "I will set a king over me, like all the nations that are round about me"; you may indeed set as king over you him whom Yahweh your God will choose. One from among your brethren you shall set as king over

you; you may not put a foreigner over you, who is not your brother. Only he must not multiply horses for himself, or cause the people to return to Egypt in order to multiply horses, since Yahweh has said to you, "You shall never return that way again." And he shall not multiply wives for himself, lest his heart turn away; nor shall he greatly multiply for himself silver and gold.'

The passage goes on to affirm that such a king must keep the deuteronomic law, 'that his heart may not be lifted up above his brethren . . .; so that he may continue long in his kingdom, he and his children, in Israel' (v. 20).

1.312   According to this formulation, Israel might at any time since it entered the land have sought from Yahweh a king, and received a king of Yahweh's choice.[22] There are certain conditions, but with one exception they are laid upon the king himself (he is to be moderate in his behaviour, and so on). The only condition apparently laid upon Israel is that the king must be an Israelite; but this condition is illogical in context, since it is Yahweh who chooses the king. Such a kingship would be hereditary (v. 20), though no such principle as primogeniture is specified.

1.32   The judge-period: Setting the terms of the 'debate'

1.320   When viewed within the Deuteronomic History as a whole, the request for a king in 1 Sam. 8 is, then, legitimate. But the theological assessment of the request, and of kingship in general, is placed in a certain light by being made to follow the long account of the judge-period. We have examined that account in detail. What, in sum, does it imply for government in Israel?

1.321   The assessment of judgeship in Judg. 2.11–1 Sam. 7 is hard to specify, in part because of the nature of the material used. In Judg. 2.11–16.31, the issues become reasonably clearly defined; the traditions used there are relatively homogeneous, and appropriate for expressing the judge-theory. Even so, the issues receive no sort of resolution there—it is unclear what ought to happen after Samson. In Judg. 17–1 Sam. 7, fairly intractable material is pressed into service to carry the issues of the debate to some sort of resolution. In Judg. 17–21, certain problematic aspects of the judge-system are permitted to come to the fore; these chapters betray concern over both continuity of government and national unity. In 1 Sam. 1–7, Eli and Samuel are subsumed forcibly under the judge-pattern, in order to take Israel, under Samuel, one last time through the whole judge-cycle.[23]

1.3221   Despite the complexity, the 'flow' of this section is reasonably clear; judgeship appears positively, then more and more negatively, and finally positively again. The section begins with the judge-system in place and working (Othniel). Then, and with increasing pervasiveness, problems with the system are permitted to appear; rule by the judges fails to conform to expectations (on the downward movement, cf. Webb: 254). First, they do not unify Israel. Tribally based as they are, they can fall into tribal rivalries in the very act of saving Israel from foreign oppresssion. The isotopy of internecine strife gives us the clearest example of *gradual* decline; beginning already with Ehud, it reaches a climax in Jephthah's war with Ephraim (Judg. 12.1-6; the theme culminates, of course, in the war against Benjamin). Second, the faithfulness of the judge may prove to be itself an issue; where lies the guarantee that Yahweh's appointed leader will turn out to be a leader in faithfulness? No judge from Gideon to Eli escapes some negative assessment. Third, and relatedly, Jephthah and Eli do not become judges by the normal divine initiative. Fourth, the judges from Jephthah on cease to deal adequately with foreign oppression (the continuance of the Philistine threat). And, going beyond these problems with the judges, there is the problem, intrinsic to the system, of the 'gaps' between judges, when anarchy becomes a threat.

1.3222   Hence, as we have seen, intimations of the possibility of a system of continuous government begin early to intrude into the text, and they grow stronger. What alternative theory might produce better results? The simplest answer offered is the system of minor judges, introduced quite briefly and blandly, but marking, nonetheless, another possibility for government in Israel. More complex is speculation about the families of judges, especially their sons; it tends towards thoughts of hereditary monarchy.

1.323   The problems of the judge-theory are not shirked, nor opposed theories repressed. On the other hand, the judge-theory is not abandoned, nor the opposed theories fully admitted. If the text shows no negativity towards the system of minor judges, neither does it provide the system with any such theological basis as Judg. 2 provides for the major judges—the minor-judge system does not really get into the 'debate'. Though a hereditary system beckons, the sons of judges are consistently faithless. Monarchy is once shown in its best light, as a guard against anarchy (Judg. 17–21; though perhaps the idea of a king, conceived in his absence, may be better than the reality!). In ch. 9, by contrast, kingship appears at its worst (and leads to something like anarchy)! Up to Samuel, we hear both the pros and the cons.

1.324   In Samuel, the judge-system is fully (and suddenly) reaffirmed. In him, the problems that have developed with the other judges disappear. He unites the people and leads them in faithfulness. He puts an end even to the long-standing Philistine threat. Samuel traditions have surely been pressed into the judge-pattern for no other purpose than to provide this glorious, final justification for the judge-system. Israel repents, the Philistines are defeated, Samuel presides over a faithful and unified Israel 'all the days of his life' (7.15)!

1.3251   Yet there is one problem which not even Samuel can solve, the basic problem of continuity. The structural basis for the judge-period gives every appearance of being a theological contrivance. Certainly nothing in the larger biblical tradition of a judge-period[24] hints at programmatic 'gaps', and such a passage as Ruth 1.1, 'the days when the judges ruled', surely assumes a continuous system. What is the theological point of the cyclical system? We have seen that there is no provision for continued leadership after the death of a judge; the rise of a new judge is a predicate of Israel's renewed apostasy. One is constrained to ask: How, then, would Israel be governed if it did not fall into apostasy? Not at all, or by Yahweh in some direct fashion? The point of the discontinuous system is, perhaps, that Israel has *freedom* for some quite new possibility; freedom which it never uses well, but which is nonetheless periodically renewed. The theory, then, would be as follows. The equilibrium situation is some kind of theocracy, undefined in detail. When Israel's apostasy disturbs this, Yahweh, after due chastisement, appoints a judge. While the judge lives, Israel will be well ruled; when the judge dies, the ideal equilibrium situation, Yahweh's direct rule, will be restored. Such a theory is never directly stated; narrative cannot develop the 'ideal' successfully, since part of the ideal is that it cannot change into the non-ideal (1 §2.212)! Yet freedom from human rule is present in our text at least as a concept. This helps explain the continuing appeal of the judge-system, and suggests that the trend we perceived towards a continuous system (§1.3222) is itself an aspect of Israel's gradual decline during the judge-period.[25]

1.3252   I do not, within the scope of this essay, intend to analyze the part of the Deuteronomic History up to Judg. 2.11; but, in relation to the 'ideal' just mentioned, one word is in order. The form of government represented by Moses and Joshua is continuous, in the sense that Joshua's succession is arranged in Moses' lifetime, and occurs at his death. Moses and Joshua are leaders by divine initiative; in general, they lead Israel in faithfulness to Yahweh (though some examination of Moses' rebellion against Yahweh would be needed); Joshua, at least, is spectacularly successful against Israel's enemies; and they lead a unified Israel. No reason is given why a successor to Joshua could not be appointed during *his* lifetime, and this system continued. The deuteronomic section Judg. 2.6–3.6 seems clearly to indicate that the Moses-Joshua form of government led into the judge-cycles without anything significant in between. This picture is, however, enormously complicated by the fact that Joshua dies twice (Josh. 24.29-30, as well as Judg. 2.8-9), which draws our particular attention to the section between the two death reports, specifically Judg. 1.1–2.5. This section is logically analogous to a 'gap' in the judge-cycles, in that Israel's situation at Joshua's death is the same as its situation at the death of any judge, with neither a leader nor a procedure for getting one. In Judg. 1.1–2.5, Israel is faithless (2.1-5), utterly divided (into tribes), and at best partially successful against its enemies. The significance of the stuttering start of the Book of Judges (a prelude before 'judges' actually appear, but a new beginning achieved through the repetition of Joshua's death) is that we get a proleptic *negative* impression of the 'gaps', militating against any interpretation of them as an 'ideal' time of direct government by Yahweh.

1.33   The *impasse* at 1 Sam. 7 and its resolution

1.331   The deuteronomic narrative is in great difficulties at the end of 1 Sam. 7. Having reestablished the judge-cycles, how can it move forward, and in particular achieve the transition to monarchy? Otherwise put, how can Samuel be the *last* of the judges, clearing the way for monarchy, *and* the one who proves the rightness and adequacy of the judge-system?

1.332   The narrative does not, indeed, entirely find its way out of the difficulties. Far too much has been claimed for Samuel in 1 Sam. 7; there is no coherence between this chapter and the Samuel traditions which follow it. He did not 'judge Israel all the days of his life' in the sense of being political leader—for there was a king! Still less did the Philistines remain subdued during his lifetime! This inconsistency suggests that the justification of the judge-system is extremely important. Samuel *has to be* the last and greatest of the judges—the need is sufficient for one of the most glaring narrative inconsistencies in the Bible to be tolerated.[26]

1.333   Nonetheless, the text does employ certain strategies to relieve the difficulties of the transition from judges to kings. The legitimacy of the request for a king in 1 Sam. 8 is underlined by its near-verbatim agreement with Deut. 17 (Veijola: 68, 116). And, as we shall examine in more detail, the *real* appearance of kingship will be deferred, and 1 Sam. 8–12 made into as much a debriefing of the judge-period as an introduction to the monarchy (§1.36).

1.334   But without doubt the most violent means for achieving the transition is the inclusion of 8.1-3. This is the sort of passage which encourages me to think that I am getting somewhere with my methods! It is quite unexpected, yet quite necessary for the text's quasi-logic. Since Samuel has created the narrative problem, it is in him that it must be resolved (the procedure is similar to the one I identified in Jonathan—he is the essential term in the resolution of a problem which, at first sight, he seems only to aggravate; Vol. I/1). At his moment of glory, Samuel appoints his worthless sons to succeed him. Is this not a sort of solution to the problem of how judgeship can come to an end at the moment of its vindication? It self-destructs! The judge-system brings itself to an end by trying to make itself permanent through heredity; the old opts for the new. The people's seeking a king, which Samuel opposes as the negation of what he has stood for, is no more than a reprise of his own initiative![27]

1.34   The theological clash in 1 Sam. 8–12

1.341   In the remainder of 1 Sam. 8–12, the two systems of government are kept in the picture together, and a (usually implicit) comparison of them is pursued. One side of the comparison appears in 8, 10.17-19, and 12. Despite the permission given in Deut. 17, the people's request for a king is a rejection of Yahweh (8.7; 10.19; 12.16-20). The king will be (8.10-18), or at least may be (12.15, 25), bad for Israel. Samuel continues as Israel's leader in faithfulness to Yahweh, thus justifying the system he represents, and making the new one unnecessary at best. More specifically, the text has him reaffirm the adequacy of judgeship to deal with Israel's military problems (12.9-11). This point of view is ascribed to Yahweh (8.7; 10.18) and not merely to Samuel himself.

1.342   Yet such a point of view cannot explain why a king *must* be bad. Deut. 17 certainly considers the *possibility* of bad kings, and the royal shortcomings envisaged in chs. 8 and 12 are quite closely related to those which Deut. 17 mentions. But might not Israel's king be good and faithful in the deuteronomic terms? (Ch. 12 even considers this possibility, e.g. v. 14.) And, in fact, the text has nothing bad to say about the actual king. Systematically, the Saul of chs. 9–11 is presented positively *in the terms established as positive by the judge-system* (§1.2; on the contrast of all this with chs. 13ff., §1.36). The means of his becoming king preserves divine initiative. He is a leader in faithfulness to Yahweh (whereas Samuel's faithfulness has been called in question by 8.1-3!). He is successful against foreign enemies, but in circumstances much like those of the judge-deliverers. He unifies Israel, avoiding the temptation to royal tyranny. And, perhaps most striking of all, he does not appear as a dynast; the only sons in chs. 8–12 are Samuel's (8.1-3, 5; 12.2!)

1.35   The issue of foreign oppression

1.351   We may specify the 'debate' between judgeship and kingship more closely by looking at one particular issue, that of foreign oppression. 1 Sam. 12.12 is a useful starting-point. Samuel refers back to Saul's overcoming of Ammonite oppression in the preceding chapter (11). We may question, though, how, within the logic of the judge-system, this oppression could have occurred at all during the lifetime of Samuel the judge. What Samuel claims is that it was on account of their fear of the Ammonites that the people first sought a king. This claim flies in the face of ch. 8, but it suggests a quasi-logical explanation of the Ammonite threat; the demand for a king in ch. 8 was *the apostasy which starts a new judge-cycle* (cf. the similarity of 8.8, 'forsaking me and serving other gods', to the standard apostasy formulae), and the Ammonite oppression the consequent punishment!

1.352 But if some such judge-logic is functioning in the narrative, so is an opposed royal logic, within which the issues may be looked at in a wholly different way. Samuel's argument stresses the adequacy of judgeship to deal with foreign threats. But why do foreign threats occur? Because the judge-system provides an opening for them, in the 'gaps' which are an intrinsic feature of the system. The judge does a fine job of removing a threat under which the people have already suffered for years! But perhaps an entirely different system would allow Israel to escape from foreign oppression altogether. Part of what the people desire in 1 Sam. 8 is a *permanent* military capacity. It is in terms of this royal logic that Saul seems to be presented.

1.353 The issue of foreign oppression is clearly an important one in the debate between judgeship and kingship. Each offers a programme for dealing with it, and each suggests that the other is *responsible* for foreign oppression, and could at best claim to solve a problem which it brings about itself! In the judge-logic, the tendency to make leadership continuous leads to continuous oppression (cf. the compounding of the later judge-cycles under Philistine oppression); and the desire for kingship is just such national apostasy as leads to oppression as a divine punishment. In the royal logic, only a continuous system of leadership can offer continuous protection, and this becomes one of the main justifications of kingship.

1.354 This sort of analysis seems to me quite damaging to the prevailing historicist understanding of the Deuteronomic History (the same point emerged regarding the Philistines in 1 Sam. 13-31 in my essay on 'Jonathan'; Vol. I/1 §3.13). Israel's enemies need not be viewed in any realistic historical terms; 'foreign oppression' has become simply a theological variable. As the judge-cycles themselves suggest, Israel's relations with foreign nations are an *externalization* of its situation before Yahweh.[28] The basic problem in Judges and 1

Samuel is not how to deal with foreign threats, but rather how to deal with Israel itself under Yahweh.

1.36 Conclusion to Part 1

1.361   McCarthy (1973) saw 1 Sam. 8–12 as achieving a theological reconciliation between judgeship and monarchy. This is over-optimistic, but it is based on a correct insight. 1 Sam. 8–12 is *looking for* compatibility between judgeship and monarchy. The process begins with the very inclusion of these chapters on the rise of monarchy within the deuteronomic account of the judge-period (the placing of the deuteronomic division at ch. 12, rather than at ch. 7; cf. §§0.21, 1.132). These chapters succeed in affirming both systems, but in different ways. The strengths of judgeship are affirmed without regard to its intrinsic weaknesses (which could be exploited in order to recommend monarchy). Monarchy, at least in the person of Saul, is also affirmed, but less for its intrinsic strengths than by the standards of judgeship. At its inception, monarchy is to be 'tamed' by a reconciliation with judgeship. The greatest claims made for monarchy are in relation to foreign enemies; but this is precisely where judgeship is most energetically defended (§1.35)! 8.11-18 makes us expect Israel's first king to be a tyrant, but ch. 11 turns him into a judge!

1.362   But the 'reconciliation' is achieved only at a cost. None of the 'textual strategies' would work without the *tour de force*, achieved in 8.1-3, whereby the section gets off the ground (§1.334). And Saul is built up as a positive figure only at the cost of considerable tension between this section and chs. 13–31; in virtually every respect (faithfulness, success against foreign enemies, tyranny, dynasty, cf. §1.342) there is a sharp contrast between 1 Sam. 8–12 and what follows.[29] 1 Sam. 8–12 is, then, deficient as a treatment of the range of issues related to government. However, as the next part of this essay will show, the Deuteronomic History has compensated in advance for some of this deficiency!

2. *The text within a text: Judges 6–9*

2.0   Kingship in Israel makes its definitive appearance in 1 Sam. 8, and we have considered at length the theological dynamic there. But, in relation to that section, Judg. 6–9 cannot fail to hold particular interest. Standing as part of the account of the judge-period, which account, I have argued, provides the theological context for the rise of monarchy, the Gideon-Abimelech chapters record a previous time when Israel took up its deuteronomic option to seek a king. We have here, then, a proleptic treatment of the theme of monarchy. In this section, I shall offer a close analysis of these chapters (concentrating on 8.22–9.22). In the next (Part 3), I shall consider the implications of these chapters for our reading of 1 Sam. 8–12.

2.1 The Gideon-cycle and its conclusion

2.11 Gideon's judge-cycle reaches its apparent conclusion at 8.28 (for the formulae, cf. especially 3.30). I shall come back later to certain aspects of the earlier parts of the cycle, but the material of special interest to our theme begins at 8.22. The Israelites approach Gideon with an offer of hereditary rulership (the verb is *mšl*, more general than *mlk*, 'be king'). Gideon refuses the offer, and specifically rejects the hereditary principle (v. 23); he does so on the ground that human monarchy impugns that of Yahweh (cf. 1 Sam. 8.7). But in the immediately following verses (24-27) he proceeds to *act like* a king, and, in the terms of Deut 17, like a *bad* king. He accumulates as much gold as he can (Deut. 17.17b), and as a result turns away from Yahweh, leading Israel astray (Deut. 17.20a).[30] A little later, he will 'multiply wives for himself' (vv. 30-31, Deut. 17.17a). There is some irony in the closure formulae of v. 28, for a judge should guarantee in his lifetime not only freedom from foreign oppression, but also faithfulness to Yahweh.

2.12 A new cycle seems to begin at 8.33, with the regular formula (cf. 3.7; 12; 4.2, etc.). The intervening verses, 8.29-32, are thereby highlighted, as appearing to belong to neither cycle. They include information about Gideon's offspring and his burial. Such information is not a feature of the standard cycle, but is normal in the accounts of the minor judges (Richter, 1966: 237). These verses are also, as it turns out, essential to set the stage for ch. 9.

2.13 To summarize, 8.22-32 complicates the characteristic end to a judge-cycle by introducing (a) an offer of kingship by Israel to Gideon, and his refusal, (b) his acting the part of a bad king, and (c) particular attention to his progeny.

2.2   The Abimelech traditions (excluding Jotham)

2.20   For reasons which will appear, I wish to read 8.33–9.57 initially without reference to Jotham, omitting, that is, 9.5b, 7-21, 57b.

2.21   The new cycle which apparently begins at 8.33 does not proceed in the normal way, with an account of Israel's being sold into the hand of an oppressor. Nowhere in the traditions about Abimelech is there anything of foreign oppression (§2.424). This is why, in Part 1, I viewed the whole of 8.33–9.57 as relating to point 1 of the cyclical scheme (§1.1132); as providing, that is (along with chs. 17–21) a picture of Israel's apostasy in the 'gaps'. 8.33-34, with its standard reference to apostasy, fits in perfectly with this interpretation. But an unexpected feature is added in v. 35, when Israel is blamed[31] in that it 'did not show kindness to the family of Gideon in return for all the good that he had done to Israel', the syntax implying that this failure was *part of the apostasy*. We shall need to consider just what this unpaid debt to Gideon's house may be (§2.4222), since nothing in the standard judge-cycle implies any obligation to the surviving family of a judge.

2.22   Abimelech plots with his kin in Shechem to gain rule (*mšl*) over Israel (9.2). But it is surely significant that, as he does so, he seems to *assume* the hereditary principle, suggesting that the only available alternatives are rule by *all* Gideon's sons, or rule by *one*. The text implies that a form of rule was being exercised by Gideon's seventy sons (cf. Soggin: 160, 169, and §2.3441). When he has made himself into an only son by the killing of his half-brothers, Abimelech is made king (9.6). (One of the half-brothers, Jotham, has of course survived, but I am omitting the Jotham passages from the present stage of analysis.) The root *mlk* is used in v. 6; in v. 22, however, in the notice of Abimelech's reign, we find the unusual root *śwr*.

2.23   During his 'kingship' (9.22-57), Abimelech seems to enjoy a measure of success. But it ends disastrously, and reasons why are given in vv. 56-57a (omitting the Jotham reference in v. 57b); as retribution for Abimelech's crime of fratricide, and for 'the wicked-ness of the men of Shechem' (in abetting his rise). His reign is judged negatively,[32] and this experiment in kingship peters out, for Abimelech is succeeded by no heirs.

2.241　Before moving to the Jotham passages, three points should be made about the Gideon-Abimelech material just presented. First, an 'all Israel' perspective has been overlaid on what no doubt were local traditions. So far as Gideon is concerned, the all-Israel perspective belongs to the logic of the judge-cycle (8.28; cf. 33-34), and it is *Israel* which invites Gideon to rule (v. 22), and *Israel* that he leads astray (v. 27). It is also Israel which fails to 'show kindness' to his family after his death (v. 35). The tension between local and national is no doubt stretched to breaking-point in the case of Abimelech, but this only makes the insistent all-Israel perspective the more noteworthy (vv. 22, 55).

2.242　Second, there is tension in the text as to whose initiative led to the monarchical experiment. It was the people, unambiguously, who in 8.22 invited Gideon and his descendants to rule (though Webb: 226 notes how, in the Gideon-cycle as a whole, there is a thick interweaving of Gideon's and the people's motivations). With Abimelech, the ambiguity is deep. Superficially, he came to power by his own initiative (9.1-5), the people acknowledging a *fait accompli* (v. 6). But this perspective is reversed by 8.35—it is the people that is in general responsible for subsequent events—and the final verdict in 9.56-57a sees responsibility on both sides (§2.4223).

2.243　Third, and anticipating my later isotopic analysis (§2.42), it is striking how the Gideon-Abimelech material, recounting as it does the story of Israel's proto-monarchy, abounds with indicators, some direct, some more oblique, of the themes of heredity and monarchy. From the outset, it is to a *family*, as much as to an individual, that we are introduced. Gideon identifies himself by family (6.15), and his father, Joash, has a significant role in the action (6.25-32). Family matters reappear in the remarkable paragraph 8.18-21; we are here told of an incident not previously recorded, in which the Midianite kings executed Gideon's brothers. The killing of these Midianite kings is therefore an act of *family* vengeance. Quite gratuitously, so far as the narrative is concerned, 8.18 tells us that Gideon's brothers 'resembled the sons of a king', and this must set Joash in a kingly perspective. Joash (2 Kgs 11-14; cf. note 40) and also Jotham (2 Kgs 15.32-38) are names to be borne by future kings in Israel; and the name Abimelech, whatever its technical meaning may be, surely invites in context the literal understanding, 'My father is a king'.[33]

2.3   Jotham and his fable

2.311   I turn now to the Jotham material (9.5b, 7-21, 57b),[34] particularly, but not only, to his speech in vv. 8-20, including his fable. Jotham is not merely a name attached to a fable, he is a character in the narrative, and one who considerably alters its dynamics. I shall deal with the impact of his introduction below (§§2.336, 2.43), but one initial point may be made. Jotham's voice coincides in a special way with the voice of the narrator (so Polzin, 1980: 174). This may be seen first by comparing 8.35 with 9.16b; Jotham's implication in the latter verse that the people have not done right by Gideon has already been directly stated in the narrator's own voice. 9.57b affirms that the whole course of events has reached its divinely appointed conclusion in line with Jotham's words. Particularly interesting is 9.7, a verse which has attracted surprisingly little comment. Jotham assumes the voice of authority; 'Listen to me!' (which Boling: 172 compares with the prophetic 'Thus says Yahweh'). Not altogether clear are the words 'that God may listen to you'; the Shechemites have made no address to God. The meaning seems to me to be 'Give attention to the implications of what I am about to say, and then you will be in tune with the divine will in this matter of kingship'. If this is correct, Jotham makes a large claim to divine authority.

2.312   Some methodological tangle has grown up concerning the interpretation of Jotham's fable. Most scholars believe that it was not composed originally with the present context in mind, and I have little doubt that this conclusion is correct. Some go on to offer interpretations of the fable in detachment from context. This is a correct and important move, but not if it is made to the exclusion of other readings. The fable *is* in a context, and needs to be interpreted there. It should be read first in detachment from context to establish (in a preliminary way) a range of tolerable meanings, and thus set constraints on what it could mean in *any* context. But the present context must then be allowed to suggest which of this range of tolerable meanings are exploited. In fact, study of the context will likely go further, and suggest aspects of the fable not previously considered. Conversely, the fable will suggest how to read the context. My approach will be analogous to the one I used in 'Ahab's Quest' (Vol. I/3), namely an analysis of the 'exchange of meaning' between text (the fable) and context without prior assumption that one is the signifier and the other the signified. The reading needs to be without prejudice, and the danger of 'overinterpretation' has to be courted, since one cannot determine what is overinterpretation until one has done it! Bits of meaning float around in both text and context like charged particles. Some of them attract each other and undergo chemical change (others seem to remain inert!).

2.313 There are, in fact, two levels of context, and I shall for convenience refer to vv. 16-20 as the 'application' of the fable, and keep 'context' for the narrative context of Jotham's whole speech. Before moving to the fable, let us note some connections between the application in vv. 16-20 and the larger context. I have mentioned already the links with 8.35 and 9.57b, which make it clear that, despite the double conditional with which his speech ends (vv. 19-20), Jotham in no way leaves open the right assessment of the people's actions. We know already that they have *not* acted 'in good faith and honor'; v. 19 is irony, and v. 20 is equivalent to a curse (cf. v. 57). It is important to note that Jotham addresses himself entirely to the people, and at no point to Abimelech (even though it is from Abimelech that Jotham fears retribution, v. 21). Thus Jotham's contribution belongs very much (in terms of the tension described in §2.242) to the aspect of the text which sees the whole monarchical experiment as a transaction between God and *the people*. He goes so far as to accuse the people of killing his brothers (v. 18), an act which the context (vv. 1-5) ascribes to Abimelech (though he had the people's support).

2.320 We turn, then, to the fable. But v. 15, the most overt point of juncture between fable and application, presents such special problems that a careful procedure must be adopted. In this section (§2.32) I shall first consider vv. 8-14, and then ask how v. 15 can be read as their conclusion; what are the possibilities for reading this verse intrinsically to the fable? Then (§2.33) I shall relate fable to application, using v. 15 as a starting-point.

2.321 A society (the trees) desire to have a king over them. They set out to choose one of their number for the office. Three are approached in turn, the olive, the fig, and the vine, and all refuse. Finally, the trees offer the kingship to the bramble. Certain suggestions may be made even before we move to v. 15. Presumably the three trees first approached are those which the society of trees perceive as most fitted for office. They are recognizable in human perspective as *useful* trees (Soggin: 175, Richter, 1966: 284), and it is their sense of their own usefulness which leads them to refuse the kingship (accepting Boling's translation of the verb *ḥdl*: he translates [116], 'Have I ceased making my oil?', v. 9, and correspondingly in vv. 11, 13). These trees have something more useful to do than become king! In the same perspective, the offer to the bramble is absurd.

2.322   I agree with the many scholars (e.g. Richter, 1966: 285, Soggin: 174, 177) who see the fable as intrinsically anti-monarchical; not only do the useful trees reject kingship for themselves, they suggest a negative view of the *desire* for a king. Kingship is, in their view, unproductive, even parasitic. The absurd offer to the bramble is, in this interpretation, a confirmation of the trees' folly in seeking a king.[35]

2.323   There is no compelling reason why the fable, read in this way, might not stop at v. 14. But in fact it continues in v. 15. A great many scholars assume that v. 15a implies the bramble's *acceptance* of the offer of kingship. This is surely wrong; the bramble's words are ironic (so Lindars: 356-57, Fritz: 140). It recognizes the offer as absurd, and, doubting its sincerity (on 'in good faith', §2.333), responds with a joke: 'take refuge in my shade' is an evident impossibility.[36]

2.324   The remainder of the bramble's reply (v. 15b) is less clear. If the trees are making fun of it, the bramble desires to become a source of danger to 'the cedars of Lebanon' (no doubt the idea is of the brush fire that spreads to trees). It is the 'cedars of Lebanon' that are unexpected. In some sense, clearly, the reference is to a part of the society of trees, or, by synecdoche, to the whole of it. Cedars are particularly imposing trees, and in a fable context very similar to the present one (2 Kgs 14.9) a cedar of Lebanon has a *royal* connotation. May not the bramble be suggesting, then, an overturning of the proper order of precedence in the society of trees, perhaps even a destruction of 'natural' royalty, or rather, on account of the plural 'cedars', aristocracy? Such an interpretation coheres extremely well with the rest of the fable. But the switch to 'cedars' continues to offend by its abruptness, and I shall have to return to it from another direction (§2.334).[37]

2.325   To summarize, the fable's intrinsic judgment on kingship must be negative, especially if we are to make sense of v. 15 in relation to vv. 8-14. To seek a king, at least within a society possessing a natural order of precedence (based on usefulness or dignity) is inappropriate, and to do so by going against that natural order of precedence is absurd. In its reply, the bramble not only recognizes its own absurd inadequacy for kingship; it sees also that such a ludicrous offer can lead to no good for the society of trees.[38]

2.331   As we turn to the relation of the fable to its application, the obvious place to begin is with the studied parallels between v. 15 and the rest of Jotham's speech, specifically vv. 16a, 19b, 20:

15.   If *b'mt* you are anointing me as king over you, (A)
then come and take refuge in my shade; (B)
but if not, (C)
let fire come out of the bramble and devour the cedars of Lebanon. (D)

16.   . . . if *b'mt wbtmm* you have dealt in making Abimelech king . . . (A')

19.   . . . then rejoice in Abimelech, and let him rejoice in you; (B')
20.   but if not, (C')
let fire come out of Abimelech, and devour the citizens of Shechem, and Beth-millo; and let fire come out of Shechem, and of Beth-millo, and devour Abimelech. (D')

To display the parallels more clearly, I have omitted vv. 16b-19a, which supplement v. 16a by providing an attachment of Jotham's speech to its context.[39] Verse 19 returns to the conditional sequence by means of a resumption of v. 16.

2.332   The parallels are based on analogy between the bramble and Abimelech, and between the society of trees and the people who made Abimelech king. The situations, though, are not analogous, in that in the fable v. 15 is a response to a present offer, while the parallel in vv. 19-20 expresses a judgment on an action already taken. There is a further tension between the parallels, which may be expressed as follows. The alternative conditionals in vv. 16a, 19b-20 each represent a genuine possibility, given the respective conditions (though obviously Jotham's speech is loaded in the direction of the negative condition):

> If this king-making was well done, (A′)
> then may king and people have mutual joy; (B′)
> if not, (C′)
> then may king and people cause mutual ruin. (D′)

Irony is certainly present, but it is all in A′; if A′ held, then B′ would apply. In the fable, on the other hand, B carries most of the irony; it is less a real outcome than a *reductio ad absurdum*. The condition in C, furthermore, is unreal; why should the trees make an *insincere* offer? It seems obvious that the alternative conditionals in v. 15 have been constructed artificially, on the model of those in vv. 16, 19-20.

2.333   Several further points can be made about the parallel sequences. First, A-A′. The expression that I have left untranslated has in v. 15 a shorter, and in v. 16 (cf. 19) a longer form (a hendiadys). The longer form is translated in RSV 'in good faith and honor', and by Soggin 'in good faith and honourably' (172). This seems more contextually right than 'with complete honesty' (Boling: 166; cf. NEB), for the issue of *honourable* behaviour does arise in the Shechemites' treatment of Gideon's house. The meaning of the shorter form in the fable (v. 15) seems, on the face of it, to be 'sincerely' (cf. NEB, 'really'; Soggin: 171, 'in truth'; and the comment of Moore: 248, 'not jest and mockery, but serious earnest'). The use of virtually the same expression in fable and application conceals a difference in logic between the two cases; the parallel has in fact been accomplished by means of a word-play (cf. Veijola: 113).

2.334   The parallel B-B′ is reasonably close, on the one hand the people enjoying the king's protection, on the other king and people finding mutual satisfaction. In D-D′, the parallel between 'cedars of Lebanon' and 'citizens of Shechem' is not immediately comprehensible. The cedars in the fable are, I have supposed, exalted members of the society of trees; it is hard to link this with the Shechemites, except conceivably as a hint that the Shechemites have chosen their own *inferior* as king over them (cf. 9.28). A suggestion of Lindars (359) may, however, be helpful here. He reads the end of v. 15 as an originally independent proverb, 'Fire comes out of the bramble, and consumes the cedars of Lebanon', the point being 'A small spark can kindle a huge blaze'. If such a proverb existed, it is not incredible that the presence of the bramble in the fable, together with the theme of fire in v. 20 (itself composed in relation to vv. 46-49), might have brought it to mind as a punch-line for the fable. The technique seems inept, since the proverb is rather robbed of its 'point', the verb has to be construed as jussive, rather than indicative, and the parallel between fable and context becomes less than precise. But the general point common to fable and application is clear enough: 'May this whole monarchical experiment blow up in your faces!'.

2.335   As many have noted (e.g. Richter, 1966: 249, 251), the main break in the parallelism between fable and application is the *reciprocity* in B' and D' between Abimelech and the Shechemites—the possibilities are *mutual* joy and *mutual* ruin—which has no parallel in B and D. Why is mutuality significant in the application? We have noted already (§2.313) that Jotham's speech concerns the people rather than the king, so that one might expect the application to parallel the fable by concentrating on the effect Abimelech will have on the people (rather than *vice versa*). But the role of the people is important, and I shall return to it below (§2.422).

2.336   There remains one point arising from the parallel between fable and application, but it is much the most important. Indeed, it is on a different *scale* of importance from the preceding, but it has remained unnoticed. The analogy between the bramble and Abimelech is obviously basic to Jotham's speech; much of the message comes from the fact that the bramble 'is' Abimelech. But in an equally important sense, the bramble 'is not' Abimelech. The bramble is the *speaker* of 9.15, and, as such, parallels *Jotham*, who speaks the corresponding words in vv. 16-20. In my earlier parallels, the 'me' of A could not be reproduced in A', for there it would be Jotham, not Abimelech! The bramble fully understands the situation in the fable; it knows its unworthiness, and the potential for ruin if the trees should elect it as king (this follows from my earlier conclusion, 2.323, that the bramble does not, in v. 15a, accept the kingship, but ironically rejects it). The bramble combines the features of 'being unworthy' and 'understanding the situation'. In the application, and in the light of the larger context, these features can no longer fall together; the former belongs to Abimelech, but the latter to Jotham. Jotham's fable creates a double allegory; an overt allegory based on bramble = Abimelech, and a covert one based on bramble = Jotham. In my view, the most profound literary effect of Jotham's fable is to open up the narrative significance of its speaker. But to explore its significance, we must now move to the relation of Jotham's whole speech to its narrative context.

2.341   We have now examined Jotham's speech intrinsically, and considered in particular how a part of the fable (v. 15) may have been formed by the need to make it parallel to the application. Our next question is, how the speech, and in particular the fable, suggests a reading of the context. The answer may, of course, suggest adjustments in the reading of the fable. There are some powerful tensions between fable and context. Richter (1966: 249), confining his view of the 'context' to 9.1-5a, 6, has laid out some of the main tensions: in the context, Abimelech's initiative—in the fable, the initiative of those who would have a king; in the fable, free choice about whom to invite to be king—in the context, Abimelech's *fait accompli*; and the lack of attention in the fable to the alternative of *oligarchy* which the context seems to envisage (rule by the seventy, v. 2; cf. §2.3441). I reject, of course, Richter's supposition that it suffices to regard the fable as of separate origin, and therefore simply to interpret fable and context independently; and I think he takes a too limited view of the context. But my analysis must deal with the tensions he (along with others) has noted.

2.342   The fable is about an approach made by a society with a view to *beginning* a monarchy, and the only parallel to this in the context is 8.22; the context with which the fable resonates must begin at least as early as this. Gideon, like olive, fig, and vine, rejects the approach; I defer for the moment the significance of his refusal. Nonetheless, the story of Israel's monarchical experiment goes forward; and the text suggests that Gideon himself is in part responsible for this. For the possibility that one of Gideon's sons might become king is raised by his illegitimate son Abimelech (9.2)—a product of Gideon's 'multiplying wives for himself' (Deut. 17.17)!

2.3431   Abimelech's words in 9.2 are skilful. They initially imply that rule by one of the seventy *legitimate* sons would be better than rule by all of them (§2.3441). Only in a subsequent, cryptic sentence does Abimelech reveal his own ambition (Jehu's ploy in 2 Kgs 10.1-5

is quite remarkably parallel—note especially the wording of v. 3!)[40]
But is there not a hint here that Abimelech, like the bramble in the
fable, comes at the end of a *series* of worthier candidates? The seventy
legitimate sons are not, certainly, presented as a series. But their
slaughter 'upon one stone' implies their elimination one by one (in
this connection the account of David's selection by Samuel, 1 Sam.
16.6-13, resonates loudly, if discordantly!). But the series concept
extends further, across generations. Gideon belongs to the series of
prospective kings, and the text goes out of its way (8.18-19) to present
even *his* father, Joash, and his dead brothers, in a kingly light.
Abimelech is very much the end of a series. This is what kingship,
once begun, comes (or may come) to.

2.3432   But why, specifically, is Abimelech, like the bramble, an
unworthy end to the series? One thinks first of the fratricide, but this
will not quite answer; the unworthiness ought to be intrinsic to his
being. 9.18 suggests very strongly that his unworthiness, in comparison
with the seventy, lies in his *illegitimacy*. Such a line of thought leads
inevitably back to Jotham (§2.336). His survival means that Abimelech
is not, after all, Gideon's only remaining son. A *legitimate* heir lives!
The conclusion of the monarchy line of thought in our text is Jotham.
But he does not reappear, even after the usurper is dead (though he
will be the last character to be mentioned in ch. 9!).

2.3441   Before moving on, it is necessary to explore a little more the
oligarchical alternative raised in 9.2. It is interesting that the term
posited over against kingship in ch. 9 is not judgeship but oligarchy.
There may be a connection here to *minor* judgeship; one thinks of the
interest shown in the offspring of certain of the minor judges (Jair, 30
sons, 10.4; Ibzan, 30 sons and 30 daughters, 12.8; Abdon, 40 sons and
30 grandsons, 12.13). The link with Gideon is striking—the big,
round numbers, the total of 70 offspring in the case of Abdon, and the
apparent rulership function of Jair's sons, who 'had 30 cities'.
Perhaps the possibility is in mind of an aristocracy of city chiefs. But
the text provides no theoretical elaboration of such an oligarchical
dimension in the minor judges, any more than it does of the minor-
judge system in general (§1.323). Two other texts may be drawn
upon for 'intertextual' clues. 2 Kgs 10 knows of seventy sons of a
king. There is no suggestion of any joint rule, however; the issue is
the choosing of *one* of them as king. Of some interest, nonetheless, is

the fact that the problem raised by a king's having many sons arises
in a context similar to Judg. 9.[41] More distant, but more appealing, is
Num. 11, to which I devoted a study in Volume I (I/2). Moses, feeling
that the leadership of Israel was too great a burden for him to carry
alone, asked assistance from Yahweh (vv. 14-15) and ostensibly
received it in the form of seventy prophets. But the experiment came
to nothing, and it was my conclusion that the narrative judged
Moses' request for assistance negatively. In that text, at least, rule by
a group of seventy was judged negatively over against rule by one.

2.3442   Can we draw any parallel between the rule of the seventy
and the fable? We may approach the question by considering: What
was the *status quo ante*, in the fable and in its context? In the context,
9.2 implies that the seventy sons of Gideon were exercising rule in
some aristocratic way. In the fable, the most worthy among the trees
were taking care of their proper spheres of responsibility. I have
suggested above (§2.324) that the fable presents the society of trees as
possessing a natural order of precedence (the 'cedars of Lebanon'),
and that the suggestion of kingship is an unwelcome intrusion into
this aristocratic order. The connection in this respect between fable
and context seems to be much stronger than commentators have
noticed; both fable and context suggest the superiority of oligarchy/
aristocracy over monarchy (cf. Crüsemann: 40).

2.4   Kingship in Judg. 6–9

2.41   Kingship or no kingship?

2.411   In the perspective of the Deuteronomic History, Israel in its
land *may* have a king (Deut. 17.14-15); such an initiative may be
dangerous, but it is within bounds. Is the people's approach to
Gideon (8.22), then, 'legitimate', as I argued the people's initiative in
1 Sam. 8 to be (§1.320)? A problem arises in Gideon's being their
own choice, not Yahweh's, in contravention of Deut. 17. One might
reply that Gideon has already been demonstrated as Yahweh's
chosen within the logic of the judge-cycle; nonetheless, a question
remains.

2.412   Most of the subsequent text moves within the logic of Israel's
having sought a monarchy and got one (I summarize the earlier

discussion). The end of Gideon's career receives a decidedly monarchical cast,[42] and it is suggested that Gideon's seventy sons exercised a form of rule. Abimelech's succession and reign are judged negatively, but this (as we shall see more clearly) is on account of his fratricide and other misdeeds, and on account of his illegitimacy, rather than on anti-monarchical principle. And monarchical 'clues' have been strewn about—the names Joash, Jotham, and Abimelech, the royal theme in 8.18-21, perhaps the closeness of Judg. 9.1-6 to 2 Kgs 10–11.

2.413   But there are features of the text which do not fit the logic of a legitimate proto-monarchy: first, Gideon's refusal of the people's offer of kingship (8.23); second, the anti-monarchical tenor of Jotham's fable, Jotham being, as we have seen, spokesman for the narrator (§2.311); third, the absence of any monarchical claim on behalf of Jotham, though he is logically the legitimate heir; fourth, and perhaps above all, the fact that this monarchy—despite the intrinsic continuity of monarchy—comes to an end. Of these, the first is the most startling, creating in the text a direct contradiction between Gideon's refusal and his subsequent depiction as king. Some have thought to solve the problem by interpreting Gideon's words in 8.23 not as a rejection but as a polite form of acceptance (Crüsemann: 43 gives a list of proponents of this view).

2.414   It seems to me better to think of the text as being overloaded at this point with the contrary messages it must convey. A notion which has been explored in recent fiction is that of alternative futures—futures dependent upon different choices made at a critical moment—existing together, and even impinging upon each other (Borges: 44-54; Russ). Our text keeps in play the futures dependent upon Gideon's acceptance of the kingship, and upon his rejection of it. The future dependent on his acceptance is the overt topic of the narrative—Israel's proto-monarchy proceeds. But the future dependent upon his rejection continues to obtrude, both formally and materially. Formally, we may refer to 8.28, 33-34, which belong to the standard judge-cycles. Materially, if Gideon does not become king, the period of the judges will continue. This, in fact, is what eventually happens after Abimelech. Unlike the monarchy which Samuel will inaugurate, the one established by Gideon will revert to rule by judges. How this can come about, by what 'logic' a monarchy—

intrinsically continuous—can come to an end, I shall consider below
(§2.43). First, I shall consider what gets *said* about kingship as a
system of government, particularly in relation to judgeship, through
the recounting of this proto-kingship in Israel (drawing again on the
isotopies used in Part 1).

2.42   Isotopic analysis

2.4211   Our text assumes *heredity* to be intrinsic to kingship. But
since kings (especially those bad ones who 'multiply wives') have
many sons, the question arises of which son succeeds. At this point,
the text introduces a fresh possibility, that of rule by *all* the king's
sons, as an oligarchy or aristocracy (§2.344). Hereditary rule does not
have to be *mon*archy. The text seems to have some positive interest
in this alternative; however, it does not receive sufficient development
to become a significant term in the debate over government.

2.4212   In relation to monarchy itself, our text certainly does not
affirm *primogeniture* as the appropriate hereditary principle; it seems
rather to go to extremes to discredit it. The family tree in Judg. 6–9
looks as follows:

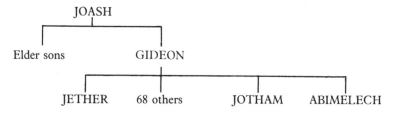

Gideon is chosen above his elder brothers (6.15), who will predecease
him (8.18-19). In the only reference to a first-born son, Jether fails
the test set him by his father, of executing the Midianite kings (8.20).
In the next generation, the youngest son (Jotham) again outlives his
elder brothers (having the wit to hide himself from the slaughter,
9.5). This is a kingship based as little as possible on primogeniture; at
every level youngest sons are preferred, indeed only they survive to
be heirs at all!

2.4213   Legitimacy is affirmed over illegitimacy, particularly in 9.18
('the son of his maidservant'). The legitimate is made to speak the

curse, eventually effectual, upon the illegitimate. The possibility of 'palace' intrigue centred on the mothers of contenders to the throne is hinted at (9.1, 3).

2.4221   The issue of *initiative for kingship* is of great importance. Deut. 17 allows for an initiative of the people in the first beginning of kingship, but the choice of king must be left to Yahweh's freedom. The situation is complicated in the case of Gideon; the people request as *king*, on their own initiative, the one who has already become *judge* by divine initiative! There is no indication at all of *divine initiative* in the succession of Abimelech; he becomes king because his father was king (cf. his name!).

2.4222   The tension in the Abimelech account is between the people's initiative and Abimelech's own. From this perspective, Jotham's speech (9.7-20) appears in a peculiar light. The fable is strongly anti-monarchical, but it concerns the first beginning of monarchy (the Gideon, not the Abimelech, situation). The rest of the speech complains, not that the people have chosen a king, but that they have chosen the *wrong* king, stressing in particular Abimelech's illegitimacy (v. 18). Once monarchy is in place by the people's initiative (Gideon), it cannot—even from an anti-monarchical point of view—simply be ended by the people's initiative. Yet the people have a responsibility in regard to *which* of the king's sons assumes the throne! This rather unexpected message is reinforced by reference to the larger context. In 8.35 (§2.21), Israel is blamed for not showing to Gideon's family, after his death, the 'kindness' that his merit deserved, and it is this dereliction which, in Jotham's speech (9.16-19), is identified with making Gideon's illegitimate son king. The conclusion must be that the unspecified debt to Gideon's house (8.35) was to accept its ongoing rule, but that the people failed to monitor the hereditary system properly!

2.4223   It is in this light that we can understand the strong, and up to now unexplained, pressure in the text to stress the people's initiative and to downplay Abimelech's own (§§2.242, 2.313). Abimelech's tyrannical behaviour is not unimportant, but what is to be stressed is the people's responsibility in the face of tyranny. The subsequent account in ch. 9 stresses the people's role in getting rid of the tyrant.

2.423   No special point is made of Abimelech's effect on *Israel's faithfulness* in a cultic sense; but, of course, the effects of his reign are deplored in general, and his whole career stands under the rubric of Israel's renewed unfaithfulness (8.33-34). More interesting is *Gideon's* leading of Israel astray, coming as it does directly after his refusal of the kingship. Despite the narrative inconsequence, a link is established between the appearance of the hereditary principle and the judge who leads Israel into apostasy (§1.2122 on Eli and Samuel).

2.424   As to *foreign oppression*, Gideon the judge defeats the foreign oppressor in the normal way. But it is exactly at the moment when his victory is complete that he receives the offer of kingship and then falls into apostasy. It is, indeed, by means of the spoil taken from Midian (and particularly from its kings, 8.26) that Gideon errs. Kingly glorification in victory seems to be linked with Israelite unfaithfulness. There is no further foreign oppression during the time of Gideon or Abimelech; but it would be facile to suggest a 'message' here that kingship preserves safety from outside aggression. More important in relation to Abimelech is *internecine strife*. The king foments internal conflict, on account of the inter-group jealousies his succession arouses, and he creates distance between himself and his subjects by his tyrannical behaviour.

2.43   The 'worthy refuser'

2.431   The people may get rid of a tyrant, but not of a monarchy in place. How, then, could Israel's proto-kingship have 'lawfully' come to an end? The answer lies in Jotham, but only as the most important aspect of a discernible 'message' in the Judges text; a rather extreme 'solution' to the problem of kingship. Given that Israel's king must be chosen by Yahweh (Deut. 17.15), the 'solution' is that anyone worthy of Yahweh's choice would be worthy enough to refuse! Conversely, anyone not worthy enough to refuse must necessarily become a bad king.

2.4321   This message is carried ambiguously by the figure of Gideon. Having been found worthy of kingship (in terms both of divine attestation and of Israel's acclaim), he makes the proper pious refusal (8.23). But there is difficulty with this. His narrative role is to function as a term in a 'legitimate' proto-kingship. Therefore he has to be a king, despite his refusal. The immediately subsequent portrayal of him as a bad king (in the terms of Deut. 17.14-20) provides what is needed (8.24-27). A narrative inconsequence is hard to deny (though one might ask whether the narrative is not credible psychologically—Gideon cannot decide which future to opt for!).

2.4322   It is interesting to consider this very basic ambiguity in the figure of Gideon in relation to the well-known problem of his two names (for the following, cf. especially Polzin, 1980: 169-70). He is sometimes called Jerubbaal; exclusively so in ch. 9 (after his death), rarely in chs. 6–8 (for analysis, Soggin: 103). The narrative makes expressly clear that the two names belong to the same person. Commentators speculate on the likelihood of two separate traditional heroes' having become compounded; but most, for purposes of exegesis, ignore the differentiation. Polzin suggests that the double name reflects a 'split characterization' of Gideon, 'a basic tension concerning his loyalty towards Yahweh' (1980: 169). The element 'baal' in his alternative name is certainly suggestive; though 'Jerubbaal' has been given an anti-baalistic etymology in 6.25-32, it is used most frequently in ch. 9, in the account of the 'bad' consequences of Gideon's career (and cf. the appearances of 'Baal' in 8.33–9.6!). It is also worth remembering that dual names are particularly characteristic of *kings* (cf. Soggin: 104).

2.433   Jotham's fable carries the message of the refusal of kingship by those worthy of it in a perfectly clear way, with the nuance that kingship is parasitical on the body of the nation (Buber: 75, Veijola: 113). But what of Jotham himself? It seems to me he is the greatest 'worthy refuser' of all. His survival constitutes a problem for our text. Logically, we are left with a surviving 'king' in succession to Gideon. He is doubly desirable as heir—youngest son and legitimate. But he does not assume the kingship; he is 'left over' at the end as the surviving scion of a line which goes nowhere. Having spoken against kingship in his fable, having spoken the effective curse on Israel's proto-kingship (9.56-57), he restores judgeship by disappearing! Having been established, inevitably, as the legitimate heir, he simply absents himself, so that judgeship may resume. The comparison is unavoidable with my view of Jonathan (Vol. I/1). The 'illegitimate' shift from the house of Saul to the house of David could there be made plausible only by the abdication of a legitimate heir, and this

Jonathan accomplished. Jotham abdicates too, but more radically; he opens the future not to another monarchy, but to no monarchy at all!

2.44   Conclusion to Part 2

2.441   Judges 6–9 has turned old traditions into a theological statement about kingship in Israel, by the imposition on the traditions of an 'all Israel' perspective. The whole section takes a perceptibly anti-monarchical view, not merely in including anti-monarchical traditions, but particularly in the narrative's identifying Jotham's anti-monarchical position with its own (§2.311). Nonetheless, and despite the problem of the people's initiative in 8.22 (§2.411), it seems to treat the proto-monarchy as *legitimate*, and therefore as needing to be theologically resolved.

2.442   The section treats many aspects of monarchy, with particular stress on its potential evils. It assumes kingship to be hereditary, and says or implies much about heredity, its 'rules' and its problems. Through what is said both about Gideon and about Abimelech, the characteristic misdeeds of kings are rehearsed.

2.443   Despite its anti-monarchical cast, the section does not assume that a 'legitimate' monarchy can be brought to an end even by the choice of those who established it. A theological rationale must be found for a monarchy's coming to an end. The solution is the 'worthy refuser'; Gideon contributes to this solution, but it is embodied in Jotham.

3. *Conclusion*

3.11   At the close of my analysis of 1 Sam. 8–12 (§1.36), I noted how that section, in chronicling the definitive appearance of monarchy in Israel, failed to deal adequately with the theory of monarchy, and concluded that this was due to a need to reconcile monarchy with judgeship. Aside from 8.11-18, no specific problems were raised concerning monarchy; and Saul was portrayed positively, to an extent that appeared artificial in relation to the very different assessment of him from 1 Sam. 13 on. Monarchy having come to Israel permanently, despite the rightness and sufficiency of judgeship, it was necessary to downplay the aspects of monarchy which, in relation to judgeship, were new and dubious.

3.12   1 Sam. 8–12 thus betrays the need for another view which it itself cannot express because of the constraints it is under. I wish to suggest that, within the totality of the Deuteronomic History, Judg. 6–9 provides that other view proleptically. If the whole narrative of the judge-period prepares us generally to read 1 Sam. 8–12, Judg. 6–9 does so much more specifically. The rise of monarchy has happened before! Judg. 6–9 adjusts our reading of 1 Sam. 8–12, as it were, in advance. Being under no constraint to portray kingship positively, it can explore thoroughly its dubious aspects.

3.2   Before it can do so, however, it must solve the same problem that 1 Samuel faced—how to get 'logically' from judgeship to kingship. The methods used with Gideon and with Samuel are not very different. Samuel reached the high point of his judgeship in 1 Sam. 7, immediately before precipitating the monarchy. Gideon attains the high point of *his* judgeship in Judg. 8.23, his great anti-monarchical confession, immediately before acting the part of a bad king. The narrative inconsequence in Judg. 8 is sharp, but hardly sharper than between 1 Sam. 7 and 8.1-3!

3.31   How, then, does Judg. 6–9 impinge on the reading of 1 Samuel? (A) In contrast to 1 Sam. 8–12, monarchy in Judg. 6–9 is overtly *hereditary*. Hereditary monarchy is in principle a direct negation of divine initiative in the raising of Israel's leaders. But this may be obscured in accounts of the *founding* of a monarchy, since there is no problem about Yahweh's choosing the *first* of the line (in 1 Samuel, indeed, a way is found for Yahweh to choose the first *two* kings). Abimelech provides an example of the fact, unavoidable in the long run, that kings become kings not by free divine choice, but by being the sons of kings. (B) The Saul of 1 Sam. 8–12 in no way threatens Israel's *faithfulness to Yahweh*. Gideon's kingship, on the other hand, is synonymous with his leading Israel astray (8.24-27). (C) Saul is a *unifier* who avoids playing the tyrant. The experience with Abimelech, in contrast, makes clear that kings provide no guarantee against internal strife, that tyranny is typical of them, and that people under a monarchical system must guard against tyrants!

3.32   Point by point, then, Judg. 6–9 opposes the view of kingship embodied in the Saul of 1 Sam. 8–12; it is circumstantial where the latter is schematic or deficient, and mostly negative where the latter is mostly positive. Samuel, in 1 Sam. 12, despite being the champion of the judge-system, leaves open the possibility of kingship's being a success: 'If both you and the king ... will follow Yahweh your God, it will be well' (v. 14). When Jotham employs the same conditional (Judg. 9.15, 19), it is with deep irony, and with no thought of an open future.[43] Judg. 6–9 fills a niche in the Deuteronomic History; it meets the need for a proleptic treatment of kingship. It provides an anticipatory variant to the rise of monarchy in 1 Samuel, adopting a different view, and with a different outcome.

3.4 There is much in Judg. 2.11–1 Sam. 12 whose significance becomes clear only later in the Deuteronomic History, and the scope of my treatment needs to be extended to take in the whole work. For example, Judg. 8–9 becomes a veritable dissertation on monarchy (§2.42). It deals with all the problems of the multiplicity of royal offspring—primogeniture, legitimacy, usurpation, palace intrigue focussed on the king's wives—matters not unfamiliar to Israel, according to the later part of the Deuteronomic History, but irrelevant through 1 Sam. 12. Nonetheless, the section up to 1 Sam. 12 (§0.21) has certainly proved important enough to merit a special treatment, and we may conclude by asking what, finally, it 'says' about leadership in Israel.

3.51 Leadership by judges brings Israel close to direct rule by Yahweh. It represents an ideal, especially since, in its inherent discontinuity, it from time to time throws Israel back *immediately* upon Yahweh. But such closeness to Yahweh is dangerous for human beings, who tend to misuse freedom; the judges themselves are not immune from corruption. However, the judges vision is not to be quickly discarded—the faithful judge remains a possibility, and under such a one Israel may again find faithfulness and blessing. Judgeship remains Yahweh's direct will in a way that kingship is not.

3.52 Kingship offers continuity, and a buffer for Israel from the impossible freedom. But it is always the result of human initiative, in which Yahweh acquiesces, rather than Yahweh's direct will. Yahweh is willing to let go of the reins, and leave Israel to the results of its choice. But what will those results be? That depends on the king. He may embody all the best qualities of the faithful judge, like the Saul of 1 Sam. 8–12. Or he may be a tyrant. The absence of a king may be intolerable (Judg. 17–21). So may the presence of one (ch. 9).

3.53 But is there any point in an open 'debate' between judgeship and monarchy? Monarchy is inherently continuous, even guaranteed by Yahweh; this belief is deeply ingrained in the traditions about the house of David (2 Sam. 7). Once in the system, then, Israel will surely have to take what it gets. But this proves not to be quite so; monarchy, once begun, can end. The Gideon-Abimelech episode offers the only example, but it suffices; if Israel's proto-kingship came to an end, then kingship in general can come to an end. This is surely a contribution of some importance to Israel's theologizing about government—not only theoretically, but in the real life situation of the Exile.

3.54 The end of the proto-kingship was accounted for by the idea of the 'worthy refuser', embodied especially in the figure of Jotham (§2.43). This idea of the worthy refuser gains a foothold even in the traditions of Saul's rise; 1 Sam. 10.21-24 juxtaposes the themes of his visible worthiness for kingship (vv. 23b-24) and his reluctance to become king (vv. 22-23a). Saul, as we have seen, is in general portrayed in chs. 8-12 not much differently from a judge. Does not this incident suggest that he might have remained a judge? The worthy refuser theme indicates how monarchy, despite its being licit and requested by the people, might never have begun (cf. also Gideon), as well as how, once begun, it may come to an end (Jotham).

3.55 Our text, then, militates against any royal fatalism in Israel. A striking parallel has here emerged (§2.433) to my piece on Jonathan (Vol. I/1). In David, Israel received a royal system that was permanent, an everlasting dynasty; but, just before this was established, the impossible possibility of a royal dynasty's coming to an end was achieved by means of Jonathan's 'abdication'. In our text, even more profoundly, before Israel receives its permanent *form* of government, monarchy, the impossible possibility is achieved of monarchy itself coming to an end, by means of Jotham's 'abdication'.

3.6 The Deuteronomic History is neither pro-monarchic nor anti-monarchic (cf. Webb: 228-29), nor (Buber: 83) 'balanced' between the two. It lets monarchy be seen for good and bad, and judgeship for good and bad; it also (though not very clearly) lets other possibilities be seen. Out of these elements, Israel is free to create its 'political theology'!

Chapter 3

'THE JORDAN A BOUNDARY':
TRANSJORDAN IN ISRAEL'S IDEOLOGICAL GEOGRAPHY

> But in order to go from east to west, they will first of all have to
> cross the river. The latter has both a dividing and a unifying
> function . . . (Lévi-Strauss, 1978: 440-41).

> Does the construction of these traditions around the Jordan . . . not
> suggest that the conquest theme was recast in accord with the
> prejudices of the people of Canaan (Coats: 188)?

0. *Introduction*

0.1   An intersection between literary structuralism and sociohistory?

0.11   A decisive impulse for this study came from a footnote in
Norman K. Gottwald's *The Tribes of Yahweh*:

> There appears to be a measure of conjunction, as yet largely
> unexplored, between the linguistic context isolated by structuralism
> and the sociohistorical context, in the sense that each points to a
> larger structure of regularities that finds expression in particular
> texts. For the moment, social psychology may be the sphere in
> which the structural linguistic and the sociological approaches
> initially intersect (720).

These words (and the note from which they are taken) make clear
that Gottwald is sensitive to the importance of structural literary
methods, and wants to find some 'intersection' between them and his
own programme.

0.12   There is indeed a pressing need for models of Hebrew Bible
research capable of giving to biblical historians and to exponents of

synchronic methods some sense that they are engaged in a common enterprise. But whereas traditional biblical historiography seems not to have found a language in which to talk to structuralism, Gottwald's sociological approach provides him with one. For example, the contrast between 'synchronic' and 'diachronic' approaches has been pivotal in twentieth-century sociology. Gottwald expounds this debate, with a view to developing a more adequate biblical historiography (592-649), and himself attempts an ambitious synchronic-diachronic model for the biblical texts which he believes relevant to the reconstruction of Israel's early history (100-14). Or again, he approaches texts as the 'symbolization' of 'structures':

> In short, the historico-symbolic appropriation of history character-istic of early Israel leaves us with the task of analyzing the processes involved in such historicizing symbolism, on the one hand, and the task of trying to uncover, insofar as we can, the underlying structure and detail of the lived experiences in a framework of documented history, on the other hand (85).

Structuralist biblical scholars find Gottwald, in these and other ways, speaking our language; and, furthermore, recalling us to our theoretical roots, for the fact that structuralism grew up as inter-disciplinary, at least among the human sciences (e.g. Lane, De George) is not always obvious in narrowly conceived literary exercises. It is thoroughly structuralist to build theory about how sociohistorical reality becomes 'inscribed' in literary texts, and to read texts, as Gottwald insists on doing, in relation to sophisticated sociological models.[1] We cannot but take a keen interest in the 'intersection' which Gottwald proposes.

0.2   The question of the text

0.21   But a reading of *The Tribes of Yahweh* suggests that the intersection is some way off. What Gottwald does with the biblical text bears in practice little resemblance to what literary structuralists do with it. One of the most fundamental differences is over the 'diachrony' of the biblical text itself, that is, hypotheses about its having passed through earlier forms before reaching the present one. Gottwald determines the parts of the text relevant to his period (1250-1050 BCE) by the traditional methods of historical criticism. He lists them precisely (47-59), and deals with them virtually to the exclusion of 'later' parts of the text. His project thus begins with a decimation of what structuralists generally take as their text, that is, its final form.

0.22   It must be admitted that the 'final form' has become something of a fetish for structuralists (along with literary analysts of other stripes), and that the arguments have often been more polemical than illuminating. Regardless of what may be decided about the study of other literature, literary study of the Bible must take up some position towards the undeniable diachrony of its text. One option would be to perform comparative structural analysis of a number of hypothetical 'stages' in a text's development, 'J' for example. Such an approach might prove valuable (§0.32), and may indeed be a logical development of Gottwald's programme. Certainly there is nothing in structural methods to preclude their being applied to any agreed text, including hypothetical earlier forms of a given text. But this approach will not, surely, satisfy a structuralist; for there must be something fundamentally wrong with a project which calls historical criticism deeply into question, but which lets historical criticism define its textual object.

0.23   Are there alternatives? Does structuralism have anything autonomous to say about the diachrony of the text? Little that has been methodologically developed; but a polemical remark of Güttge-manns (49) offers a starting point: 'In principle, a "redaction" can only "insert" materials into a structural framework where the . . . sequence "grammatically" permits this from the start, since otherwise "nonsense" would occur'. He accepts, for the sake of argument, the process of 'redaction' of 'sources' posited by historical criticism, but claims that any redaction is under semantic constraint. Into the sentence 'There is a box on the table', I can introduce an adjective, perhaps 'large'. But I must put it before one of the nouns. The semantic 'grammar' of texts, Güttgemanns is claiming, imposes an analogous constraint. Loosely stated, the redaction's point of view exists only in relation to the source's point of view. We need not suppose deep-structural identity—complications, even reversals, can be achieved. But even if, for example, the *literati* who may be responsible for the P redaction should have attempted to *reverse* the JE point of view, their *having done so* would not go unrecorded in the text, any more than a person's change of mind on a matter goes unrecorded in his/her further utterances on the matter. This means that, to be true to itself, structuralism must be involved in the framing of the diachronic theories. The diachrony of the text will be 'inscribed' in its final form not only through the clues of vocabulary, style, theological point of view, and so on, to which historical criticism attends, but also *structurally*, that is, at the level of deep assumptions.

0.24   It is one thing to affirm this, another to carry it through. I do not know of any attempt, theoretical or practical, to develop Güttgemann's hint (though Polzin's treatment of certain historical-critical classics as structural analyses is of interest, 1977: 126-202). What I am implying about Gottwald is that his immense project ought to be undertaken backwards. First should come a sociohistory of the *final* form of the text, relating *its* literary structure to the 'structure of the lived experiences', and then hypotheses could be framed about what earlier texts and attitudes the final form might represent a response to. The aim would be a Gottwaldian sociohistory of the entire period of the development of the biblical text, carried out at each stage in relation to literary analysis. Only with temerity do I sketch such an enormous task on the basis of, at this stage, purely theoretical considerations. Let me add, however, and in homage, that it takes on some sense of feasibility, enormous as it is, from the work that Gottwald has done already.

0.3   The theme and scope of the analysis

0.31   I shall attempt to answer (or rather, sketch some approaches to answering) the following question: *What viewpoint does the Bible reveal towards the idea of Israelites living east of the Jordan?* I developed this question before reading Gottwald, and it is not directly suggested by him; but it touches on his work in two ways. First, it responds precisely (if I have understood him), to his suggestion that social psychology might be a point of intersection between his work and literary structuralism. My question is one of social psychology, and I believe the results indicate that the *isotopic* analysis of texts is particularly well adapted to the raising of social psychological issues. Second, Gottwald's problematic of immigration *vs.* revolt models of Israel's origins implicates Transjordan— immigration being mainly conceived as from this direction—so that ingrained attitudes towards the east ought to be related to a deep sense of whether the east did have some special significance for Israel's origins. The relation of this study to Gottwald's work will, however, be oblique; to my mind, necessarily so. For Israel, the problem of its national origins was highly fraught; and we are dealing with 'official' texts, one of whose functions is to obfuscate such dangerous issues. We need to employ a correspondingly devious style of analysis! In my conclusion (§3.2), I have summarized what I see as some potential implications of my study for Gottwald's programme.

0.32   The immediate point of departure is Num. 32 and Josh. 22, for of the many passages relevant to my question, only these two seem to have as their textual function the 'answering' of it. I have attempted a detailed analysis of these two chapters, but beyond them I have imposed considerable limitations on the analysis. I confine myself for the most part to the narrative sequence in Num. 20–36 and to some extent in Joshua. Deuteronomy, though it occupies an important position enclosed within the conquest sequence, and provides parallels to much of it, I have largely neglected; it needs its own full analysis, which would have made the chapter too long (in §2.210, I use part of Deuteronomy heuristically). Particularly where the analysis is paradigmatic rather than syntagmatic (above all in §2.1; for the distinction, Introduction §5.3), I have made use of some material from entirely different parts of the Hebrew Bible. In general, and for the reasons already indicated (§0.2), my text overlaps little with Gottwald's texts; in particular, only a few verses of Num. 32, and none of Josh. 22, are among his sources. In the earlier version, however (Jobling, 1980a: 205-206), I included a sketch of how my analysis might have differed if it had been based on JE, rather than on the given biblical text. My conclusion was encouraging: 'The later redactors have tightened the semantic organization, and have made the status of Transjordan more deeply questionable. But at every point, the structures they reveal are detectable also in the JE redaction' (206).

0.33   Part 1 is the analysis of Num. 32 and Josh. 22. Part 2 explores three diverse but typical approaches to the Transjordanian issue. Part 3 is summary and tentative conclusions. After the work was complete in its earlier form, I realized that the Jephthah-cycle in Judges would provide a test of its usefulness, and this test is carried out in Part 4 of the present version. There is a small measure of artificiality in excluding all the Jephthah material from the main analysis, but this was necessary to preserve the value of the test-case.

1. *Analysis of Numbers 32 and Joshua 22*

1.01   Num. 20.21-35 told of the Israelite conquest of some Transjordanian land. Num. 32 tells of the desire of certain Israelites to be settled in this land, rather than in Cisjordan, and how this was granted, provisional upon their assisting in the coming Cisjordanian wars. Josh. 22 takes up the account after the successful completion of these wars; a conflict has to be resolved before everyone's territorial desires are fulfilled. The group which settles to the east of the Jordan will be referred to here simply as the Transjordanians (it is convenient to leave for Part 2 issues related to the constitution of this group). Those settling in the west will correspondingly be called the Cisjordanians.

1.02   Considering the amount of material between these two chapters, it is striking how nearly seamlessly they join together. All that is needed to link them is something like: 'The Transjordanians were as good as their word. After the settlement in the west was successfully completed . . . '. In fact, there are two included passages, Josh. 1.12-18 and 4.12-13, which belong to the story-line of Num. 32 and Josh. 22, but which do not contribute much to the analysis.[2] The object of analysis in Part 1 is, then, Num. 32 + Josh. (1.12-18; 4.12-13); 22. But this object falls into separate stories, each well-formed in the sense of moving from a conflict to its resolution:

>Story I: Num. 32 + Josh. (1.12-18; 4.12-13); 22.1-8
>Story II: Josh. 22.9-34

Story I tells of the Transjordanians' desire to be settled in the east, of the conflict thus created, of an agreement made, and of the carrying out of its terms by both parties; the Transjordanians get their wish, but conflict is averted. Story II tells of a unilateral act by the Transjordanians, the building of an altar, of the conflict thus created, and of the provision by the Transjordanians of a satisfactory explanation; they achieve, apparently, what they set out to, and conflict is averted. The point of division, between Josh. 22.8 and 9, is less than perfectly obvious (cf. the analysis), but can be justified in a preliminary way by the following observations: Joshua, a significant character in

Story I, especially at the end of it, last appears in v. 8; 'the people of Israel' first appears as an actor in v. 9; the setting in Shiloh is first specified in v. 9.

1.03   The two stories will first be analyzed individually (§§1.1, 1.2); then their relationship will be analyzed, paradigmatically and syntagmatically (§§1.3, 1.4). §1.5 attempts to specify the semantic message in an isotopic analysis (for the terminology, see Introduction §§5.2, 5.3).

1.1   Story I

1.11   The main story-line. I shall at this stage bracket the reference in Num. 32.8-13 to the story told in Num. 13–14 (and also certain features of 32.14-15 necessary for the inclusion of this story). I shall return to the enclosed story in §1.12.

1.111   Story I is readily segmented, mainly by the speeches:

Num. 32.1-5		Request by Transjordanians
	6-7, 14-15	Angry response by Moses
	16-19	Compromise proposed by Transjordanians
	20-24	Guarded agreement by Moses
	25-27	Reaffirmation of good faith by Transjordanians
	28-30	Moses gives instructions to implement the agreement later, if Transjordanians prove their good faith
	31-32	Reaffirmation of good faith by Transjordanians
	33-42	Moses gives land to Transjordanians
Josh. 1.12-18, 4.12-13		Carrying out of the agreement
Josh. 22.1-8		Joshua confirms the gift of land to the Transjordanians, and dismisses them

The biggest problem brought out by this segmentation is the degree of repetition in the story. It is clearest in the double reaffirmation of good faith by the Transjordanians, but, even before this, Moses' speech in vv. 20-24 is repetitive of vv. 16-19. The following analysis must give some account of the repetition.

1.112   In Num. 32.1-5, the Transjordanians make a logical suggestion. It is reasonable, in the circumstances, for them to make their home in the east. Their request has two parts, (a) to be settled in the east, (b) not to be made to cross the Jordan *now*.

1.113   Verses 6-24. Moses responds (vv. 6-15) with great anger, seeing the request as a threat to all of Israel, and suggests no possibility of compromise. It is noticeable, however, that it is only to part (b) of the request that he objects; no one in the story, in fact, overtly objects to (a) or impugns its logic. The Transjordanians (vv. 16-19) offer a compromise—(a) but not (b). They *will* cross the Jordan, provided only that they can first make provision for their dependents and property for the interim. Moses (vv. 20-24) accepts this, but in the form of a conditional, and with a reference to a divine sanction if the Transjordanians renege; he concludes by giving permission for the interim provision.

1.114   It is frequently a powerful tool of narrative analysis to posit a *countertext*, to tell another, usually more 'natural' story, and to ask why the given text is not this way (1 §1.23; Vol. I/3 §1.2). In the present case, the compromise put forward by the Transjordanians is so obvious as to make one ask why Moses did not think of it. The countertext, then, would have Moses responding to the request in vv. 1-5 with something like the conditional of vv. 20-24 (with a Transjordanian response like vv. 25-27 following). The countertext would, of course, avoid the jarring repetition of the text. I suggest that the text has assumed its present form because of two needs; that Moses have occasion for an angry speech, and that the initiative for a compromise solution come from the Transjordanians.

1.115   Verses 25-42. These verses contribute nothing to the agreement, which is complete at v. 24, and my impression is that the chapter has been drawn out to ring some changes on the attitudes taken by the two parties, particularly by Moses—at least, this is the effect of the present text. The Transjordanians, in their reaffirmations of good faith, do not go beyond what they promised in vv. 16-19, and the repetitiveness of vv. 25-27 and vv. 31-32 is very awkward. It is worth noting, though, that in the first case they put their own interests (v. 26) ahead of those of the others (v. 27), as they did in vv. 16-17; while in the second they perceive the agreement as having Yahweh's sanction, and put the others' interests (v. 32a) ahead of their own (v. 32b), as Moses did in vv. 20-24! The Moses sections show more decided differences, over the giving of land to the Transjordanians, and over the sanctions which may fall upon them if they renege on their promise. In vv. 20-24, Moses' tone was guardedly positive. Verse 24, by allowing the building of cities, implicitly accomplished the gift of the land. Only v. 23 referred to sanctions, which were quite general, and did not include forfeiting the land. The tone of vv. 28-30 is, in contrast, harsh. The land is not yet given (it will fall to others, after Moses' death, to implement the gift), and will be forfeit if the Transjordanians renege on their bargain (v. 30). Verses 33-42, finally, are totally positive; the land is given, in precise terms and with no reference to sanctions. These variations set up an opposition which we may formulate as the prior *vs*. the posterior gift of land. At some risk of overinterpretation, the following syntagmatic understanding may be suggested: the slight reluctance of the Transjordanians in vv. 25-27 corresponds to the negativity of Moses in vv. 28-30 and entails the posterior gift, while their enthusiastic piety in vv. 31-32 induces Moses to be positive, and entails the prior gift of vv. 33-42.

1.116   In Josh. 1.12-18, the prior and the posterior gift are kept in nice tension (noteworthy is the sanction invoked by the Transjordanians on *themselves* in v. 18, though it is not related to their land). The same is true of Josh. 22.1-6, where Joshua carries out the instruction of Num. 32.28-30; what he gives to the Transjordanians is what Moses already gave (v. 4). As a final narrative touch, giving a sense of roundedness to the whole of Story I, note the fairness of Josh. 22.8, answering precisely to Moses' appeal to fairness in Num. 32.6 (as warfare must be equally shared, so must booty).[3]

1.12   The enclosed story in Num. 32.8-13. In these verses Moses invokes the story told in Num. 13–14, of the failure to enter the land from the south. The behaviour of the Transjordanians, he claims, is like that of the spies in the earlier story who discouraged the people. Thus one story is put into a hermeneutical relationship with the other, and a paradigmatic analysis becomes imperative.[4]

1.121   That the spies' story should be retold in Num. 32 briefly and tendentiously is to be expected, but significance may still be found in the particular ways in which it is deformed. The following is a segmentation of Num. 13–14, with indications of what becomes of each segment in the retelling.

13.1-16	Choosing of the spies by tribe	
17-25	Commissioning and journey	32.8-9
26-33	Report of the spies	32.9 (12)
14.1-10a	The people are discouraged	
10b-35	Yahweh's angry response; punishment of the people	32.10-13
36-38	Exemplary punishment of spies	
39-45	Abortive attempt to enter land without Yahweh's blessing	

Remarks on this table: (A) Whereas the report of the spies in 13.26-33 was a mixed one (cf. v. 27), it is wholly negative in the retelling (knowledge of the minority report by Caleb and Joshua, and their consequent blessing, is implied in 32.12, but this is not developed).[5] (B) By far the most tendentious omission is of the people's *allowing themselves to be discouraged* by the discouraging report; this was an integral feature of the Num. 13–14 story, and its absence from Num. 32 makes Moses' argument founder. (C) The Transjordanians are threatened with no such exemplary punishment as that visited on the spies in 14.36-38. (D) The final episode, the abortive attempt, appears to have no relevance to the new situation.

1.122   One is not superficially impressed with the appositeness of Moses' allusion. The Transjordanians have not seen the land of Canaan, let alone given a negative report of it—they have made no recommendations at all to anyone. The *tertium quid* is simply the discouragement the others will draw from the Transjordanian initiative; but this is no more than an imputation by Moses, as indeed is Yahweh's anger and punishment. There is, however, more to be said. If we extend our view to the whole of Story I, we find that it has a number of structural elements in common with Num. 13–14:

(a)   The spies saw the land, and called it bad. Perhaps the point in Num. 32 is that the Transjordanians have seen what is *not the land*, and called it good; but such a point would depend precisely upon Transjordan's *not* being considered part of the Promised Land. This is an issue to which we will return repeatedly (§§1.52, 2.2).

(b)   Both stories include an agreement by a part of Israel, but for the benefit of the whole, to enter the land and return—the spies before the general entry, the Transjordanians as part of the general entry.

(c)   The premature taking of the land. The abortive attempt in
       Num. 14.39-45, which, in relation to the revised divine plan, is
       premature, may be compared with the Transjordanians'
       premature desire for settlement, before the whole land has
       been conquered and divided.

(d)   The most compelling common element is of a quite different
       kind from the above, namely the prevalence of *the security of
       children*, i.e. of the next generation. But this will be better
       taken up in the isotopic analysis (§1.53).

(e)   Both stories, finally, look to a positive conclusion long deferred.

1.123   Syntagmatically, the enclosed story is so placed as to give
occasion for Moses' angry speech, for which it provides, albeit
unconvincingly, the substance. Also, though again unconvincingly, it
provides a way of bringing *Yahweh* into Story I as a quasi-actor
(§1.6).

1.2   Story II

1.20   I shall not include here any such treatment of the stories
alluded to in Josh. 22.16-20, namely Peor (Num. 25) in v. 17, and
Achan (Josh. 7) in v. 20, as I offered of the spies' story (Num. 13-14)
in §1.12. This is on account of the extreme brevity of the allusions.
Salient features of the Peor and Achan stories will, however, be
considered in the isotopic analysis of §1.5.

1.21   If we put aside v. 9 (transitional, §1.42), and perhaps the
awkward and redundant v. 11, whose concern seems to be to make it
unmistakably clear which side of the river the altar was on,[6] Story II
is in the form of a grand chiasmus:

      (a)   10   Transjordanians build an altar
        (b)   12   Cisjordanians threaten war
          (c)   13-15a   Cisjordanians send an embassy
            (d)   15b-20   Accusatory speech by the embassy
              (e)   21-29   Transjordanians' reply
            (d')   30-31   Accepting speech by the embassy
          (c')   32   Return of the embassy to Cisjordan
        (b')   33   Withdrawal of the Cisjordanian threat of war
      (a')   34   Transjordanians name the altar

Even the central element (e) has itself a convincing ABBA form: A, invocations and oaths expressing innocence (22-23, 29); B, explanation of the altar, in two closely parallel sections (24-27a, 27b-28).

1.22 My response to such impressive structure is literary admiration, and also the question, What is being put over on me that needs all this trouble? The main problem is that v. 34 looks lost, and the reason is that it wants to be with v. 10—the naming of the altar should immediately follow its building.[7] Is it too much to suggest that the admirable structure exists to 'naturalize' the separation of these two verses, whereby alone the altar is left open to misunderstanding? At any rate, a countertext is suggested (cf. the very similar observations and suggestions of Soggin: 213-14). On the occasion of the happy parting of Cisjordanians and Transjordanians, the latter, or even both parties, thought of a problem. The Transjordanians would have conceived it in the terms of vv. 24-28, 'in time to come your children might question the status of our children'; whereas the Cisjordanians would rather have conceived it as 'living so far away, indeed outside 'Yahweh's land' (v. 19), your Yahwism, or at any rate that of your children, may become dubious'. So an agreement was made: the Cisjordanians to respect the Yahwism of the Transjordanians, and to give them access to Yahweh's sanctuary, the Transjordanians to perform Yahweh's service in the prescribed way at the Cisjordanian sanctuary (cf. v. 27); and this agreement was ratified by the building of an altar as a witness to future generations. The altar was close to the west bank of the Jordan, and perhaps was considered as belonging to Transjordan, as 'a portion in Yahweh' (v. 25), and in 'Yahweh's land'.

1.23 The existence of such an agreement appears to be the upshot of the given story, but the result is achieved through a narrative of gross implausibility (cf. not only the deferred naming of the altar, but also the curious logic whereby the Transjordanians are assumed to have founded an illegitimate Yahweh-cult to the *west* of the Jordan). The achievement of the present form of the story seems to me to be simply the assimilation of these events to those of Story I, so that it is appropriate to move directly to a paradigmatic comparison.

1.3 Paradigmatic reading of Stories I and II

1.31 In the following analysis, it is to be noted how many of the features of Story II are not features of the countertext just proposed (§1.22).

(a)   A Transjordanian initiative sets the story in motion (Num. 32.1-5; Josh. 22.10).

(b)   Moses/the Cisjordanian embassy expresses anger at the initiative. Each (particularly the embassy) goes to some lengths of implausibility to put the worst possible construction on it. And each makes use of allusions to the past to establish the case (and to introduce Yahweh into the action; Num. 32.6-15; Josh. 22.12-20).

(c)   The Transjordanians make a suggestion/response which is satisfactory, and in fact provides the substance of a bargain (Num. 32.16-19; Josh. 22.22-29).

(d)   Acceptance by Moses/the Cisjordanian embassy (Num. 32.20-24; Josh. 22.30-31).

Certain differences are, of course, not to be overlooked. The situations are different; in Story I the agreement includes a promise to be made good later, while in Story II the element of future ratification is much less specific. This may be related to the most striking contrast between the stories, namely that between Moses' hesitant acceptance of the Transjordanian programme and the precipitate readiness of the Cisjordanian embassy to be convinced. The element of the threat of war in Story II has no true parallel in Story I.

1.320   Various narrative programmes (Vol. I/2 §1.120) of the two parties (assimilating Moses to the Cisjordanians) are in play—explicit, implicit, and imputed—and it is a significant part of the analysis to unravel them.

1.321   The Transjordanians have the following aims:

(a)   To establish and permanently to maintain their residence in the east.

(b)   To maintain their identity as Yahwists, and as a part of Israel (though geographically separate).

(c) To perform as Yahwists, by duly attending the service of the sanctuary.

(d) To have a permanent guarantee of this state of affairs, through forthcoming generations.

In Story I, only (a) is stressed, and (b) implied; nothing is said about any particular mode of long-term relationship with Cisjordan. As a concession, the Transjordanians make their own a Cisjordanian programme, to get the Cisjordanians settled; this necessitates a sub-programme, to make temporary provision for property and dependents, which has some connection to (d). Story II affirms all the Trans-jordanians' programmes; and they impute to the Cisjordanians' children a (potential) programme, to deny *their* children's Yahwist identity, and to prohibit their access to Yahweh's cult.

1.322   The Cisjordanians are largely in a reactive situation, so that their programmes are to be deduced in part from their reactions to the Transjordanian ones. Obviously, they wish to be and to remain settled in the west. But they see this as depending on their religious status before Yahweh, and this status as threatened by the Trans-jordanian programmes as they perceive them. They impute to the Transjordanians some rather incomprehensible programmes; to prevent the western settlement, to make Yahweh angry, to destroy the whole people. Their main programme, essentially reactive, is to offset the wrath of Yahweh against themselves which they think the Transjordanians are causing. Although they finally fall in with the Transjordanian programmes, there is in each story at least a hint of a quite different Cisjordanian programme, and one of extreme interest; the Cisjordanians continue to hope for eventual settlement of the Transjordanians in the *west*. This programme is seen most clearly in Josh. 22.19, but also of interest is v. 33, where the war is seen as to destroy the Transjordanians' *land* (as opposed, presumably, to exterminating the Transjordanians themselves), and especially Num. 32.30, the peculiar sanction against the Transjordanians should they renege on their promise (on this, cogently, Coats: 187). Thus one may surmise that the Cisjordanians see the basic Transjordanian programme as the disunifying of Israel, and they themselves include in *their* basic programme the reunification of Israel west of the Jordan.

1.33   This paradigmatic analysis may be concluded with a note on the views the stories take of the two parties. Moses and the Cisjordanians are quick to anger and ungenerous in their interpretations; though, as we have seen, the Cisjordanians of Story II are more readily appeased than is Moses in Story I. The views taken of the Transjordanians in the two stories are in much sharper contrast. In Story I they are so accommodating that they win the reader's sympathy from Moses. That this is not the case with Story II is due to their extraordinary deviousness. If their intentions in building the altar were so honourable, why did they not make them known (cf. again the countertext, §1.22). In this light, their pious invocation of Yahweh in Josh. 22.22 definitely looks like 'protesting too much'.[8]

1.4   Syntagmatic reading of Stories I and II

1.41   The forming of the two stories into one tends to make one read each in the light of the other, and in this case the effect of Story II on Story I seems to be the greater. The Moses of Story I is claimed, as it were, as representative of the Cisjordanian position. The Transjordanian deviousness in Story II can perhaps be read back into Story I—for all their accommodation there, were they not ready to leave their fellows in the lurch? On the other hand, the Cisjordanians can grasp at Mosaic authority by adopting the Mosaic style of argumentation.

1.42   To these no doubt random remarks must be added a further point of much greater theoretical importance. Story II effects a *redoubling* of Story I, by means of a *reopening*. The technique of the reopening is worth comment. Story I is complete at Josh. 22.6; 'and they went to their homes' is grammatically, as well as thematically, a closure. In other words, 22.6 so completes Story I, with the Transjordanians back in the land of their inheritance, as really to leave no room for anything else that happened before they got there. Nonetheless, something did happen. Leaving aside v. 7a (note 21), v. 7b appears as a very studied reopening, achieved in particular by repeating the verbs 'bless' and 'send away' from v. 6. The reopening is then rendered 'innocent' by v. 8, whose *content* certainly belongs to Story I; it is as if the author prefaced v. 7b with 'By the way, I forgot to say . . . ') But the reopening, once achieved, is confirmed by the 'open' language of v. 9, '(they) left . . . *in order to go* to . . . their own

land'—allowing for something to happen on the way—by which
Story II is opened. What is the effect of this? A story of a conflict fully
and happily resolved becomes a story of a conflict which led to
another conflict. Is there not profound significance in this? Though
the conflict in Story II will itself be resolved, conflict between
Cisjordanians and Transjordanians has acquired a quality of
recurrence, which makes the narrative redoubling much more than a
matter of a factor of two!

1.5 Isotopic analysis of Stories I and II

1.51 The unity of Israel

1.511 By their initial request in Num. 32.1-5, the Transjordanians
break the *integrity* of Israel. One people about to enter one land
becomes two groups with different territorial intentions. The Cisjordanians interpret non-integrity as *division*, which means danger from
Yahweh (presumably because it may or must become religious
division). The Transjordanians are quick to negate all thoughts of
such division, and an uneasy equilibrium is attained at this point. But
the Cisjordanians are prone to ask, if Israel is indeed undivided, why
not demonstrate this by geographical integrity. Cisjordanian and
Transjordanian concepts of the nature of Israel's unity are profoundly
different.[9]

1.512 It is instructive to consider certain features of the terminology
for the two parties (here briefly summarized) used by the parties
themselves, and by the narrator. There are two basic options:

$$
\text{(a)} \quad \frac{\text{Transjordanians}}{\text{Cisjordanians}} = \frac{\text{'you'}}{\text{'your brethren'}}
$$

$$
\text{(b)} \quad \frac{\text{Transjordanians}}{\text{Cisjordanians}} = \frac{?}{\text{'the people of Israel'}}
$$

Option (a), which occurs in Num. 32.6 (Moses' first remark), and
exclusively in Joshua's speech (Josh. 22.1-8), tends to include the
Transjordanians as part of Israel. Option (b), which occurs in one
form or another almost everywhere else, excludes the Transjordanians
(the ? ought to be 'non-Israelites', though this conclusion is not

directly drawn). The occurrences of (a) frame Story I, giving to it an inclusive cast, and the occurrences of (b) in Story I do not give the impression of being deliberately 'loaded'. The occurrences of (b) in Story II *do* give this impression; even at the point of conciliation (Josh. 22.31) the 'we' and the 'people of Israel' in Phinehas's speech are hard to interpret inclusively, since the narrative reverts to option (b) in vv. 32-33. The two stories give different impressions; Story I varies its rhetoric to give a movement of unity lost and regained, while the rhetoric of Story II tends to imply non-unity throughout.

1.513   The enclosed stories have a contribution to make. If Israel's unity, on which its position before Yahweh depends, is so fragile, even a single individual, let alone two tribes and a half, can threaten it. This is the message of both the Peor (cf. Num. 25.6-18) and the Achan stories; the latter being indeed *locus classicus* for this affirmation, a point not missed in the retelling—'wrath fell upon all the congregation of Israel though he (Achan) was but one man' (Josh. 22.20). An *a fortiori* argument is implied—the Transjordanians' offense is worse than the earlier ones. Rather different is the point implied by the *exemplary* punishment of the offenders as individuals (as opposed to the general punishment on Israel), which occurs not only in Num. 14.36-38, but also in both the Peor and Achan stories. Though you Transjordanians will bring trouble on all Israel, this seems to say, be sure that you will bring special trouble on yourselves. These are particularly good examples, I think, of the rich semantic content which may be carried by even the briefest allusions in a text.

1.52   Israel's land

1.521   The very basic issue must now be formally introduced of whether Israel's Transjordanian holdings are a legitimate part of its land (for the following, Ottosson, 1969: 133-35). Story I begins with words which strongly affirm the legitimacy: 'the land which Yahweh smote before the congregation of Israel' (Num. 32.4), a part, therefore, of what has been given to Israel to conquer. But Story II questions the status of Transjordan as Israelite territory. Josh. 22.19 explicitly contrasts Transjordan with 'Yahweh's land', and raises the possibility of its being 'unclean'; v. 33 suggests that the Cisjordanians intended to destroy the Transjordanian *land* rather than its people; and v. 25, though put forward as a negative possibility by the Transjordanians, evokes the idea of the Jordan as the boundary of Israel's authentic land. Geographical bipartition is not merely non-integrity, but a basis for value-judgment. It is significant in this connection that, in both stories, the Transjordanians undertake *to cross the Jordan for the service of Yahweh*. Is it the point that those whose status as Israelites is rendered dubious by their Transjordanian residence acquire sanctity by crossing the Jordan for the service of Yahweh? Since this obligation means that they are on Cisjordanian soil only temporarily, it is a *renewable* obligation, as the redoubling of Story I by Story II underlines. This issue will be of special importance for the next section (§1.53).

1.522   Even within Story I, the allusion to the spies' story of Num. 13–14 (which itself included the element of entering the land and returning for the service of Yahweh), seemed to imply doubt that Transjordan was part of the Promised Land (§1.122). The allusions made in Story II are even more eloquent. Num. 25 shows Israel, or some element of it, tempted to *remain in Transjordan for the service of another god*. And the Achan story, in the form in which we have it in Josh. 7, shows remarkable similarity in its structural elements to Num. 13–14 (§1.121):

Sending of spies (Josh. 7.2)
Their favourable report (v. 3)
Premature, unsuccessful attack (vv. 4-5)
Complaint (by *Joshua*) (vv. 6-9)
Revelation of sin (vv. 10-21)
Exemplary punishment (vv. 22-26)

All the implications cannot be pursued, but the point of major interest is the wish expressed by Joshua in v. 7, 'Would that we had been content to dwell beyond the Jordan!', a wish for which he is not rebuked. If not crossing the Jordan is sin, then sin is in a sense equivalent to not crossing the Jordan. The presence of uncleanness makes the attempt upon the land *premature*, and only its removal will allow a successful occupation (8.1-29).

1.53   Children and women; the generations

1.531   In Story I, in Num. 13–14 to which it alludes, and in Story II, there is a concern for the coming generation which amounts to an *idée fixe* (Vol. I/2 §2.224). In Story I, the Transjordanians reiterate

the need to provide for their 'little ones' (Num. 32.16, 17, 26; cf.
v. 24), while showing almost no comparable concern for their wives
(in v. 26 these do appear, *after* the little ones; note, however, that this
is reversed in Josh. 1.14). Adult males are to risk themselves, children
are to be safeguarded, and women are scarcely an issue. In Story II,
the great concern of the Transjordanians is that their *children* may be
disinherited, and it is to safeguard the interests of the coming
generation that they take the risk of internecine warfare. In this light,
the dynamic of Num. 13–14 stands out very clear, and it is in this
connection that Moses' invocation of the spies' story has its appositeness (§1.122). The wilderness generation which refused to enter the
land did so on the grounds that they would be risking their wives and
little ones (Num. 14.3). But in Yahweh's response, it is the little ones
who become significant (v. 31). It is they, for whom such false
concern has been shown, who will be the object of Yahweh's concern.
Yahweh will uphold *their* interest in the land, while the present
generation will not see it.

1.532   In one sense, the message is everywhere the same. Authentic
provision for coming generations consists in faithfully entering the
land for the service of Yahweh, even at risk to the present generation.
This accounts at one level for the greater prevalence of children than
of women, where the safety of both is at issue (women being in any
case, no doubt, semantically akin to the coming generation). Nor is
the syntagmatic point to be overlooked that the 'little ones' of Num.
13–14 become the adult generation of Num. 32 and Josh. 22, again
underlying the element of *recurrence* generation by generation.

1.533   The Transjordanians are Israelites *outside the land*, or at
least in a dubious part of it. But their situation may be regularized by
crossing the Jordan for the service of Yahweh. This logically means
that each new generation is born in irregularity, and must *renew* its
connection with Yahweh's land. But, whether it be for war or for the
service of the sanctuary, it is only the *males* who are under obligation.
Thus while each new (male) generation of Transjordanians create a
problem which can be solved, Transjordanian women are a potentially
dangerous anomaly, dealt with, in these texts at least, largely by
silence. But we note that one of the enclosed stories, that of Peor,
raises the issue of Transjordanian women (albeit foreign women) to
paramount importance, for it was women who tempted Israel to
remain on the wrong side of the Jordan.[10]

1.6   The point of view of Num. 32 and Josh. 22

Though a certain sympathy for the Transjordanians is present, it is, not surprisingly, ultimately a Cisjordanian perspective which comes across (cf. my second superscript). This is particularly clear in the treatment of Yahweh. In Story I, Moses (except in Num. 32.33-42) and Joshua consistently make reference to Yahweh, while the Transjordanians only gradually begin to do so. In Story II, by contrast, both sides do so consistently, so that the story becomes a contest over Yahweh. This would become merely a stand-off, with neither side able to *prove* its superior Yahwism, were it not for a striking piece of narrative technique, namely the inclusion of the allusions (the spies' story, Peor, Achan). In the main narrative of Num. 32 and Josh. 22, Yahweh is not an actor; Yahweh simply neither does things nor says things. But the narrative makes Yahweh into a quasi-actor by the specific means of the included stories, for Num. 13–14, Num. 25, and Josh. 7 are all narratives in which Yahweh does and says things, and their use makes plausible the claim that he will have things to say and do in the given situations. But it is only the Cisjordanians (including Moses) who can claim Yahweh in this way, creating an imbalance in the narrative between the parties.[11] Narrative *form* is in this case more powerful than narrative *content* in carrying the 'message' of a partisan Cisjordanian claim upon Yahweh.[12]

2.   *Miscellaneous investigations into the Transjordanian issue*

2.0   In this part, three examples will be offered of fruitful lines of investigation; I have chosen them to exemplify different facets of the issue of paradigmatic *vs.* syntagmatic analysis (Introduction §5.3). §2.1 inquires paradigmatically into the significance of the *particular* tribes who make up the Transjordanians; §2.2 considers the syntagmatic relationship of Num. 32 to chs. 20–36 as a whole; and §2.3 deals, in 'the daughters of Zelophehad', with a case where paradigmatic and syntagmatic dimensions are particularly hard to separate.

2.1   Paradigmatic relations among Reuben, Gad, and Manasseh

2.11   The occurrences of Reuben, Gad, and Manasseh in Num. 32 and Josh. 22 are not symmetrical. Reuben and Gad always appear as

a pair, though in Num. 32 their ordering is odd—after being
introduced with Reuben first (v. 1), which is the usual order (Josh. 22
and almost everywhere else), they are reversed, Gad- Reuben,
throughout the rest of Num. 32. As a pair, they stand over against
Manasseh. Manasseh is, of course, only half Transjordanian, and
even the half-tribe finds no settled position in either chapter. In
Num. 32, it does not appear until v. 33, and in vv. 34-42 its
occupation of land is differently recounted, in style and in substance,
from that of Gad and Reuben; while in Story II, it disappears in Josh.
22.25 and 32-34. This basic distinction between Reuben and Gad, on
the one hand, and Transjordanian Manasseh, on the other, will recur
below (§2.24).

2.12   In the tradition of Gen. 29.31–30.24, Reuben is Jacob's
firstborn. He almost always heads lists of the tribes.[13] Particularly
interesting are Deut. 27.12-13 and Judg. 5.14-18, where Reuben
heads, not the whole list, but the subset of tribes judged negatively/
put into a negative situation. For Reuben lost his precedence by
sleeping with his father's concubine, Bilhah; Gen. 35.22 records the
act, 49.3-4 the consequence (though Reuben is still at the head of this
list). Thus the genealogies of 1 Chron. 2–8 demote Reuben with a
reference to this disgrace.[14] Reuben is mentioned quite frequently in
Genesis, and would be susceptible of an extended analysis (particularly
of his persistent relationship with Joseph); but for present purposes
he is one who *loses precedence on account of a concubine.*

2.13   Loss of precedence is no less clear in the case of Manasseh,
who in Gen. 48.8-20 is Joseph's elder son, but whom Jacob puts
below Ephraim, the younger. In the lists which include them,
Ephraim is generally placed above Manasseh, though exceptions are
found (Num. 26; 34; 1 Chron. 7.14-29). Josh. 16–17 is ambiguous. In
16.4, the order is 'Manasseh and Ephraim', and 17.1 implies that
Manasseh, as the elder, is receiving its land-allotment first; but in
fact Ephraim has received first (16.5-10)! The issue of precedence
here continues into the next generation, for in 17.1 Machir receives
precedence as *Manasseh's* firstborn. In as much as he is also the
forefather of the Transjordanian half of the tribe, some sort of
precedence is suggested of Transjordanian over Cisjordanian
Manasseh, but in a context where precedence is tantalizingly apt to
be reversed! I shall deal with this genealogy much more fully in

§2.31. Another form of the same genealogy provides the concubine connection, for according to 1 Chron. 7.14 Machir is Manasseh's son by 'his Aramean concubine'.[15]

2.14 The tradition concerning Gad is scant and featureless compared with Reuben or even Manasseh. He usually appears low in the tribal lists (the only reason for a higher place seems to be to create a link with Reuben, with the Transjordanian settlement in mind, e.g. Num. 1.24-25). Gad is, indeed, a firstborn, of Jacob's (Aramean) concubine Zilpah. But one would have no real thought of precedence in the case of Gad were it not for the extraordinary passage Deut. 33.20-21, in the Blessing of Moses. I am aware of the great critical problems here, but it can scarcely be denied that some significant precedence is ascribed to Gad. The blessing of Gad exceeds even that of Judah; at most that of Joseph equals it. The expression 'couches like a lion' (v. 20) is used of Judah in Gen. 49.9. The meaning of $r'\check{s}yt$ (v. 21) is not clear, but it indicates that Gad aspired to some sort of precedence (the RSV translation, 'chose the best of the land', would, if correct, be relevant to our discussion; but there is no obvious justification for the rendering). The obscure term $mhqq$ (cf. Moore: 153) is used in similar contexts in relation to Judah (Gen. 49.10) and, of particular interest for our study, Machir (Judg. 5.14).

2.15 Thus a link is forged between Reuben, Gad, and Manasseh (especially Machir) under the headings 'lost precedence' and 'concubine', though the concubine connection is weak in the case of Gad, in as much as Jacob had several concubine-sons. In relation to the analysis of Part 1, the element 'concubine' links up with the 'problematic' Transjordanian women (§1.533), while the element 'loss of precedence' seems so prevalent that even at the most 'microscopic' level normal orders are, as it were, routinely reversed (e.g. Reuben and Gad in Num. 32). But 'loss of precedence' has a much profounder reflection in Num. 32 and Josh. 22. Reuben and Gad grasp for precedence in the gift of land. In a sense they get it, but in another sense they go to the bottom of the list. They may receive first only if they are willing to enjoy last (cf. the prior vs. the posterior gift, §1.115).

2.2 The legitimacy of Israel's Transjordanian land

2.20 In Num. 32.4, Gad and Reuben refer to the land they want as 'the land which Yahweh smote before the congregation of Israel'—it is therefore, presumably, fair game for settlement. But some problems emerge, in the surrounding chapters (specifically Num. 20.14–36.13; for the starting-point, cf. Coats: 177-79), concerning this entitlement. §2.21 will deal with the sequence 20.14–21.35; §2.22 with issues related to Moab; §2.23 with minor issues; and §2.24 with an important distinction which emerges between Israel's Transjordanian holdings *north and south of the River Jabbok.*

2.2101   A useful approach to Num. 20.14–21.35 is via the highly stylized parallel sequence in Deut. 2.1–3.17. It falls into a pattern of non-conquest followed by conquest:

(a) Non-conquest (2.1-23). The main point is that Israel has no claim on the territory which Yahweh has given to its *affine* peoples, Edom, Moab, and Ammon (the affinity is stressed in vv. 4, 9, and 19), and it must not molest these peoples. Verses 28-29 make it clear that Israel passed through Edom and Moab (this is not made clear in vv. 1-15, though cf. v. 6).

(b) Conquest (2.24–3.11). The land of Sihon and the Amorites is to be the beginning of Israel's conquests (2.24-25), and the conquest actually takes place (vv. 31-37) after Sihon has refused Israel's request to pass through his land peacefully (vv. 26-30). 3.1-11 then recounts in a parallel way the conquest of the territory of Og, King of Bashan.

2.2102   The table opposite shows the schematic geography under-lying the text.

A number of points are in need of clarification:

(a)   Deuteronomy assumes, as we have seen, a route crossing Moab from south to north. In Numbers, in contrast, we shall find a route passing by Moab on the east.

(b)   Deut. 2.37; 3.16, in common with other texts (Num. 21.24; Josh. 12.2) make the Jabbok the boundary of Ammon. But this does not refer to the Jabbok's westerly flow (as in the diagram), but with its roughly northerly flow in its upper reaches (cf. Miller and Tucker: 100; Ottosson, 1969: 109-10).

```
                              OG

                         Half-Manasseh

                           Jabbok
         ┌────────────────┬──────────────────┐
C        │                │                  │  T
I    J   │      Gad       │                  │  R
S    o   │                │                  │  A
J    r   │     SIHON      │     AMMON        │  N
O    d   │                │                  │  S
R    a   │     Reuben     │                  │  J
D    n   ├────────────────┴──────────────────┤  O
A        │                                   │  R
N        │      Arnon                        │  D
         │                                   │  A
         │      MOAB                         │  N
         └───────────────────────────────────┘
            (EDOM far to south)
```

Key: Upper-case—Nations/their kings
     Lower-case—Rivers
     Italics—Israel's Transjordanian settlement

(c)   This scheme assumes the following equations:

$$\frac{\text{Sihon}}{\text{Og}} = \frac{\text{Gad and Reuben}}{\text{Half-Manasseh}} = \frac{\text{South of Jabbok}}{\text{North of Jabbok}}$$

While the texts do not always make these distinctions precise (to a large extent because of confusion over the meaning of 'Gilead', on which see §2.243), this is the composite picture governing them.[16]

2.211   We turn to Numbers, and first to the non-conquest sequence (cf. Deut. 2.1-23). In Num. 20.14-21, Israel makes to Edom a direct request for free passage, which is refused (Deut. 2.29 implies that this request was made, but with the opposite response). Israel therefore *circumvents* Edom, and also—as 21.10-13 is at pains to insist—Moab, with which there are no negotiations. Although, in contrast to Deut. 2.16-23, Numbers says nothing of avoiding Ammon on the journey, 21.24 makes a particular point of the fact that Israel's conquests

stopped at the Ammonite border.[17] Israel's affinity, at least with
Edom, is expressed by the 'brother' of 20.14. Though there are
differences between the two accounts, notably between the implied
routes, there is agreement on the main point that Israel is not to
trespass on the territory of its *affines*.

2.212   The conquest sequence in Num. 21.21-35 (cf. Deut. 2.24–
3.11) raises a problem which will be of the greatest importance for
our discussion, namely, the peculiarly 'accidental' quality of the
conquest of Sihon's territory. This, like Edom and Moab, lies on
Israel's natural route, and in both accounts Israel approaches Sihon
with a request entirely parallel to the one made to Edom in Num.
20.14; to pass through his land and be on its way. But this implies
that, if Sihon had granted Israel free passage, his land would not have
been conquered! Is the extent of the Promised Land, then, to be
determined by the decision of a foreign king? The treatments of this
problem in Numbers and Deuteronomy differ. What finally counts
for Deuteronomy is 'divine gift', and 2.24-25 makes clear that
Yahweh has given Israel Sihon's territory just as Yahweh has given
land to Edom, Moab, and Ammon (and will later give Og's to Israel).
The appearance of accident is alleviated by the 'hardening of the
heart' theme in v. 30 (so that the request to cross Sihon's land
peacefully was a charade, like the corresponding scenes in the Plague
traditions). The Numbers account attempts no such alleviation of the
problem; it lacks (in contrast both to the deuteronomic parallel and
to the Numbers account of the defeat of Og in 21.33-35) the divine
assurance of victory which is a correlate of the 'divine gift' theology.[18]
So far as Sihon is concerned, Numbers seems content with a 'right of
conquest', rather than a 'divine gift', point of view.

2.221   The 'accidental' quality of the conquest of Sihon's land raises
acutely the problem of the legitimacy of Israel's Transjordanian
territories (§1.52). But even if we were to accept Numbers' 'right of
conquest' approach, this would only raise a second level of problem,
namely the text's insistent sense that Israel is infringing on the
territory of *Moab* even after its defeat of Sihon. After the scrupulous
avoidance of Moab on the journey, it comes as a surprise that Israel
arrives in Moabite territory in 21.20. This might be seen as temporary,
pending Israel's having land of its own by the defeat of Sihon. But in
fact the Moabite location of the following chapters will be repeatedly

stressed (22.1; 26.3, 63; 31.12; 33.48-49; 35.1; 36.13), and, even more significantly, it is precisely *after* the defeat of Sihon that conflict with Moab (and its ally Midian) becomes a major theme (chs. 22–25, 31), so important that the resolution of this conflict will be the last act of Moses (31.2) and hence the immediate condition for Israel's crossing the Jordan.[19]

2.222   The text attempts, perhaps, another rationale for the conflict with Moab/Midian, namely that, in Num. 22–31, the problem is simply Israel's proximity to these peoples, and consequent temptation. Even if we were to accept this rationale, however, a question would still be raised over Israel's Transjordanian territories; for as long as it has them it will have dangerous neighbours! The sense is present in the text that Israel will be *safer* when it has crossed the Jordan (which fits in with Moses' extreme anger at the Transjordanians in ch. 32). But the rationale based on proximity will in any case not quite do, particularly for chs. 22–24. For here it is the Moabites who sense danger from Israel, rather than *vice versa*, a feature which is compatible neither with Israel's avoidance of Moab on the journey, nor with the idea that Israel is now occupying its own legitimate territory (won from Sihon). The sense is undeniable that Israel is on land which the Moabites regard as theirs.

2.223   The clue undoubtedly lies in 20.26, which asserts, however briefly, that some at least of Sihon's land had previously been Moabite, and that Sihon had taken it by conquest. But this completely transforms the (theo)logical situation. According to 'right of conquest', Israel holds Sihon's territory properly, as Sihon previously had. But according to 'divine gift', Israel cannot have land which Yahweh gifted to its affines—not even, presumably, when that land has since fallen into other hands. In trying to rest its case on 'right of conquest' (§2.212), while agreeing with Deuteronomy that the affines' land is sacrosanct (§2.211), Numbers gets itself into a logical cleft stick! (Deuteronomy, of course, avoids the problem by omitting the tradition that Sihon's land had been Moab's—but notice Deut. 1.5 and 29.1, in contrast to 4.46!) This line of reasoning is confirmed by the obsession with Moab in Num. 22–31, but also from a quite different direction. According to the foundation myth of Gen. 13, Abram and Lot divided the Promised Land into west and east. The details of this division are not quite clear (partly on account of the traditional location of Sodom) but in mythic logic it would tend to coincide with the best-known west-east division, between Cis- and Transjordan. Lot's inheritance would then simply be (some part of) Transjordan, and would have passed to Moab and Ammon in the continuation of the myth in Gen. 19.30-38. Israel, I am suggesting, had a sense, a mythic 'knowledge', that lower Transjordan properly belonged to its kinsfolk of Moab and Ammon. This called in question the traditions of Israel's settlement there (not to mention David's conquest of these lands within historical memory; cf. §3.23). The myth has therefore been revised, and the issue obfuscated, by the business about Sihon and the Amorites.[20]

2.224   The issue of Moabite/Midianite women in chs. 25 and 31, while not touching directly on the issue of legitimacy, is closely related to it through our earlier discussion. In ch. 25 (to which Josh. 22.17 alluded) these women seduced Israel, both sexually and religiously, and thereby, as I speculated, tempted Israel not to cross the Jordan (§1.533). Chapter 31 presupposes ch. 25. After defeating the Midianites, the Israelite force takes booty including 'the women of Midian and their little ones' (31.9)—notable is the agreement of this with the instructions for taking a city *outside Israel's territory* (Deut. 20.14-15). Moses, however, points out that it was precisely the non-virgin among these women who seduced Israel (vv. 15-16). The male children and the non-virgin women are thereupon killed, while the virgin women are kept alive (vv. 17-18). The logical problem of Transjordanian women was considered earlier (§1.533), and the present passage ties in with it. Is it the case that non-virgin Transjordanian women have, as it were, taken the contagion irredeemably, so that they are a source of danger, but so that conversely it is meritorious to bring a Transjordanian virgin into Yahweh's land?

2.231   In Num. 26, a census is taken, at the end of which (vv. 64-65) it is noted that by this time the wilderness generation was all dead. Though the time of its dying out is not more precisely specified (and note the difference of this tradition from Deut. 2.14-15), the note in 26.1 that the census was 'after the plague' invites the conclusion that the last of the wilderness generation died precisely in the plague of Peor (25.9). But this would imply that Israel was not yet in the Promised Land. In any case, Moses' own survival (cf. Coats: 189-90) has the same implication, for (as will be reaffirmed in 27.12-14) he is not permitted to see the Promised Land; he survives the wilderness generation, but only as (excepting Caleb and Joshua) its last member.

2.232   In the course of the census (26.52-56), Yahweh instructs Moses in the division of the land. The extent of the land is not defined, but the division is obviously to be to all twelve tribes. The principles of division are that it be by tribal size and *by lot*. The passage is repeated, largely verbatim, in 33.54. Two points are to be made about this repetition. First, it *follows* ch. 32, and belongs, in fact, to a large section, 33.50–34.29, whose aim seems to be the smooth incorporation of ch. 32. The new instructions have to do with the division of *Cisjordan* only, among the remaining nine tribes and a half. But this fails to conceal the irregularity of the procedure by which the Transjordanians had their inheritance determined; it certainly was not by lot. Second (and, though speculatively, of great potential importance), the repetition in 33.54 of the instructions for dividing the land is injected into a section (vv. 51-56) about the issue of *non-Israelites in the west*. They are to be exterminated along with all trace of their influence, for any who remain will cause great trouble. An important link is perhaps being created here between two issues which are superficially unrelated, but very straightforwardly related in mythic logic—the (continued) existence of non-Israelites in Cisjordan, and the existence of Israelites in Transjordan. This would provide a reason for the insistence of the Cisjordanians' desire (Num. 32.30, Josh. 22.19) that the Transjordanians to come west after all; it is room which the Transjordanians ought to be filling which is filled with Canaanite troublers of Cisjordanian Israel!

2.241   There is, however, an important nuance to the ambiguity about Transjordan, and to identify it we must return to the conquest sequences in Numbers and Deuteronomy. Num. 21.33-35 parallels to the conquest of Sihon and the Amorites that of Og, King of Bashan, whose territory lay north of the Jabbok. The parallel is made much clearer in Deut. 2.24–3.11 (cf. 3.8, 'the two kings of the Amorites'). But the parallel is weak. Sihon's land lay on Israel's route to Canaan, whereas Og's certainly does not. If crossing the Jordan is Israel's priority, then the conquest of Bashan is at least premature. On the other hand, the effect of this premature move is to make Og's territory more 'naturally' a part of the Promised Land than is

Sihon's—Israel conquers it because it is Israel's to conquer, not merely because it is accidentally in the way! Num. 21.33-35 includes the divine assurance of victory which was lacking in vv. 21-32 (§2.212).

2.242   The logical status of the two parts of Transjordan is, then, different; the land to the north of the Jabbok is less problematic than that to the south. This should mean, in terms of the equations of §2.2102, that the status of half-Manasseh is less problematic than that of Reuben and Gad, which agrees very well with Num. 32; for in that chapter half-Manasseh, appearing only at the end (vv. 33, 39-42), is not strictly a part of the earlier problematic (e.g. takes no initiative to be settled in the east, cf. Coats: 187-88). These observations invite a further speculation, that the tribe of Manasseh, in its bipartition, recapitulates and *mediates* the bipartition of Israel; Israel's being split in two is softened if there is a point at which these two are still one. In the south, Israel is divided, but in the north it is joined.[21]

2.243   By far the most common geographical term for Transjordan in the Bible is 'Gilead'. But it is extraordinarily elusive; it can be used to mean Transjordan in general, or some specific part, which may be north or south of Jabbok, or both (Ottosson, 1969: 242-53 and *passim*)! Ottosson (29) denies even that the sources suffice to determine a part of Transjordan to which the name was originally confined. As a *genealogical* item, however, 'Gilead' is firmly fixed in the Manasseh genealogy (§2.31). Israel, it seems, became accustomed to thinking of Transjordan as a single entity, and had available a name, 'Gilead', on a level with 'Canaan' for Cisjordan. But the name, and the sense of a single entity, cloak a significant difference between north and south of Jabbok; and it is noteworthy that, while it was in connection with Reuben and Gad (the more problematic part) that the issue of Transjordanian settlement first arose in the text, it is half-Manasseh (the less problematic part) which comes to stand, genealogically, for Transjordan as a whole.

2.25   In summary, the texts affirm that Yahweh 'smote Sihon's land before Israel', and at the same time renders this conquest problematic. All the above points contribute to the text's creation of Transjordan as *ambiguous land*. It belongs, at some level, to Israel; yet there is the suspicion of another level at which it belongs rather to someone else, so that Israel's occupation of it is not Yahweh's intention (this 'someone else' is Israel's affines, Moab and Ammon). But, in a final turn, the text confines this ambiguity to one part only of Israel's Transjordanian land, the area south of the Jabbok.[22]

2.3 The case of the daughters of Zelophehad

2.31 The relevant texts are Num. 26.29-33 (the Manasseh genealogy in the census), 27.1-11 and ch. 36 (the 'case'), Josh. 17.1-6 (the settlement of Manasseh), and 1 Chron. 7.14-19 (the genealogy of Cisjordanian Manasseh). Before dealing with the case, it is necessary to dwell for a moment on the genealogy.

2.311 The version in Num. 26 is as follows:

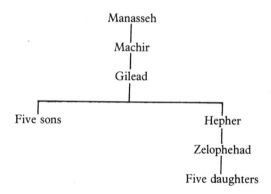

This genealogy is assumed in chs. 27 and 36. In Josh. 17, however, it seems initially (vv. 1-2) to be adjusted to put Hepher and his five brothers at the same genealogical level as Machir; that is, they are all Machir's younger brothers:

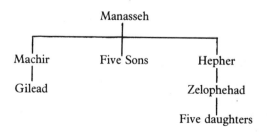

In v. 3, the genealogy reverts to the standard form, with Hepher one of the sons of Gilead.

2.312   The names of Hepher and the five sons are (with the exception of Asriel) well-established geographically as Cisjordanian, as also are some of the names of the daughters (Noah, Hoglah, Tirzah; Ottosson, 1984: 104). And the 1 Chronicles genealogy, containing many of the same names and likewise based on Machir, is presented as the genealogy of the *Cisjordanian* half of Manasseh. Ottosson (1969: 138-41, 1984: 104) concludes that Machir was historically of Cisjordanian origin. I have no quarrel with this historically, but it is not in accord with what is going on textually. Machir constantly turns up among the founders of Transjordanian Manasseh, beginning with Num. 32 itself; and he is normally the father of Gilead, whose name is also Israel's most general term for 'Transjordan' (§2.243). It will be our task to interpret the 'mythic' genealogy, in which Machir-Gilead represents Transjordanian Manasseh. The case of the daughters of Zelophehad strongly illuminates what the myth is getting at, and the syntagmatic relationships between its parts and the conquest narrative prove essential to the interpretation.

2.32   Syntagmatically, the opening of the 'case' in Num. 27.1-11 depends not only on the genealogy of 26.29-33, but also on 26.52-56, the principle of inheritance, and on 26.64-65, the death of the wilderness generation. The case is introduced, then, at the earliest possible instant, which may indicate its special importance. The daughters of Zelophehad come to Moses with a request that, since their father died without sons (as one of the wilderness generation), his name should be preserved by them, the daughters, through their receiving a possession along with their male relatives. This is granted. The entire issue of land-inheritance seems premature at this point, since no division of the land has been made. But the next part of the 'case', ch. 36, stands in a quite different light because of the intervention of ch. 32. The daughters belong to the stock of Machir, that is, to a part of Manasseh which has already received its (Transjordanian) land-allotment (32.39-40). In this new situation, the male members of the tribe raise a problem about the earlier ruling in favour of the daughters of Zelophehad. Should the daughters marry out of their tribe, it will lose the inheritances which they have been granted (making a mockery of the principle of fixed tribal divisions). The force of this is allowed, and propertied women are bound by law to marry within their tribe, which the daughters of Zelophehad in fact do.

2.33 This completes the 'case', but Josh. 17.1-6 resumes the story and sets it in a new light. How are we to interpret the shift in genealogy in vv. 1-2 (§2.311)? The revised form, first of all, rationalizes the division of Manasseh into two parts (as the standard form does not). Machir founds the Transjordanian, his 'brothers' the Cisjordanian, moiety. Second, the priority of the Transjordanian is affirmed, since Machir is the 'firstborn' (but cf. §2.13!) Third, the daughters of Zelophehad, who in Num. 36 were by strong implication Transjordanian, become unambiguously Cisjordanian![23] But the new-fangled genealogy cannot be maintained, it seems, more than momentarily, for v. 3 reverts to the normal one.

2.34 I do not pretend to offer a single logical explanation of all of this, but make the following comments with some confidence. Within Manassite traditions, there is the same evidence of worry over the issue of Cisjordanian *vs.* Transjordanian as we have found in the all-Israel traditions; the attribution of eponyms to one side or the other is inconsistent, and precedence between the two is an issue. And, particularly in the case of the daughters of Zelophehad, the question of *Transjordanian women* continues to crop up. The narrative first invites us to see the daughters as Transjordanian women (by introducing their case in Transjordan, and by relating it to Num. 32 via Machir), but later wants to make them Cisjordanian. In an odd way, therefore, the text makes them marry and move west, and this is felt to solve an urgent problem. The importance of the case of Zelophehad's daughters is to bring together the whole problematic of 'Transjordanian women' with that of the inheritance of land. Though many specifics differ, the general 'message' is very similar to that of parts of our earlier analysis (§§1.533, 2.224). What is striking is that this is all worked out within Manasseh. The tribe which mediates the problem of all Israel (§2.242) also recapitulates it. Israel is divided into two by the Jordan. But one of the tribes ensures Israel's singleness by straddling the border. But that tribe is itself divided into two by the Jordan, and *its* singleness becomes an issue![24]

3.   *Conclusions*

3.1   Summary of the findings

3.10   Our attempt to answer the initial question about Cisjordanian attitudes to Transjordan has led us into a constellation of narrative meanings which to some extent has taken convincing form and which may be considered as a symbolization of real attitudes. The conclusions may be presented under four headings.

3.11   The unity of Israel. The Cisjordanian perspective is that Israel is one integral entity, and, in this perspective, Transjordan has an ambiguous status. It is to be claimed as authentic Israelite territory; but its separation, and its inhabitants' sense of that separation, threaten territorial integrity. Thus the unity of Israel is felt to be called deeply in question by Transjordan. Along with the claim to it goes a sense of danger from it, along with the desire for a formalized relationship, the wish that it would just go away. There is a sense that Transjordan possesses some sort of precedence, in face of which Cisjordanian precedence needs to be the more strongly affirmed—we have everywhere found the literary theme of reversal of precedence relationships. The Transjordanians have an obligation to the nation as a whole, and need to be reminded of it—there is a heavy-handed maintenance of authority, which cloaks anxiety and the lack of real power. The characteristic mode of interaction between the parties is quarreling and making up.

3.12   The extent of Israel's land. A sense of doubt manifests itself that Israel has a legitimate claim to its Transjordanian lands. The claim is never, in the texts we have studied, overtly abandoned, even though abandoning it would solve the problem of territorial integrity— no doubt it is a political universal that claims to territory tend to override other considerations. In addition, we have discovered a faint hint of a whole different logical connection—a sense that Israel's problem of foreigners *within* its (Cisjordanian) territory may be correlative with Israelites' living *outside* that territory (§2.232). If only the Transjordanians would be content to take up residence in Cisjordan!

3.13   Transjordan as two separate entities. The tensions defined in the last two paragraphs are softened, or mediated, by separating Transjordan into two, and assigning different logical status to the two parts. The division is at the Jabbok, and it separates Transjordan into the territory of Reuben and Gad, to the south, and that of half-Manasseh, to the north. Doubt about the legitimacy of Israel's claim applies only to the southern portion. Manasseh itself represents a mediating element, as the only tribe living on both sides of the Jordan. Superimposed, then, on the deep sense of the Jordan as boundary, and in considerable tension with it, is a sense of less problematic relations towards the north-east, and in this context Manasseh assumes particular importance; but, at a further level, the 'all Israel' problematic can be recapitulated in Manasseh itself.

3.14 Transjordanian women. The issues have something to do with women and children. Definitions of the relationship with Transjordan lack continuity from generation to generation, and Transjordanian women present a logical problem and a danger. To marry a Transjordanian woman, so that she moves west, seems to assume positive significance; on the other hand, the traditions are full of the element of irregular or secondary marriage, 'concubinage'. In this connection, reference may be made to Malamat (132), who puts forward a literary-sociological model for the reading of biblical genealogies, including particular reference to female terms. 'Daughters . . . generally represent either clans or, rather, settlements—dependent on and subject to the principal tribal group or urban center.' 'The merging of a tribe, settling in a new area, with an earlier or indigenous population may be formulated as a marriage of the tribal eponym with one of the local women. Union with a concubine may personify a fusion with a foreign or inferior ethnic element.' ' . . . in attributing lineage through a concubine or maidservant, the Bible intends to convey the idea of migration . . . from the ancestral home to peripheral regions.' The anthropological status of such a model needs to be established, but, taking it at face value, it relates 'females', particularly 'concubines', to the meaning-elements of (socio-political) *dependency, peripherality, foreignness, inferiority, and indigenity*. These are elements which could be traced, with considerable precision, in the foregoing analysis of the views taken of Transjordan. Such metaphors as these female ones, however much they may turn into technical terms, do not become innocent of their basic semantic content, and I suggest that, at a deep level, Cisjordan and Transjordan are coded simply as male and female. Nothing so bald as this ever appears on the surface, for many other semantic elements overlie it; nonetheless, the hypothesis is worth framing that this is the semantic force most deeply charging the manifest texts.[25]

3.2   The origins of Israel

3.21   In the introduction to this chapter (§0.3), I expressed the hope that the study might illuminate Gottwald's problematic of the origins of Israel, at the centre of which is the debate between theories of non-indigenous ('conquest' and 'immigration') and of indigenous origins (Gottwald: 192-227). The main point to be made in this connection is that if Transjordan, the main focus of the non-indigenous theories, is so problematic to Israel, then it is likely that the problems have to do, in part at least, with origins. But it is worth speculating a little farther.

3.22   The analysis has revealed that there are three concepts of Israel which play a role in generating the texts:

A.   A 'narrow' view of Cisjordan as 'Yahweh's land' (Josh. 22.19), and therefore as comprising the full extent of the 'real' Israel. Ottosson (1969: 240-41) ascribes this view to priestly circles. The most extreme expression of it is Ezek. 47.15-20 (but cf. Num. 34.1-12). In my analysis, the Cisjordanian attitude betrays a hankering after this solution.

B.   A 'wide' view which claims for Israel all of its traditional Transjordanian land, conceived as a unity.

C.   An implicit middle view, perceiving Israel as consisting of Cisjordan plus Transjordan north of the Jabbok. The unstated bases for such a view are the integrity of the tribe of Manasseh and the less problematic appearance of Israel's claim to north than to south Transjordan.

To venture a large simplification, A and B are, in Gottwald's terms, 'conquest', that is non-indigenous, views, while C is an indigenous view. This statement has both textual and historical aspects. The difference between the two conquest views is expressed by Coats (186) as the difference between Numbers and Deuteronomy; the deep implication of Deuteronomy is that legitimate conquest begins at the Arnon (B), of Numbers, at the Jordan (A). I call view C 'indigenous' on the sort of grounds put forward by Ottosson (1969: 190-92). Northern Israel always felt a stronger attachment to Transjordan than did Judah, and there is plenty of evidence that northern Transjordan was settled, beginning at an early date, from northern Canaan. We may therefore posit an early 'Israel', in the north but on both sides of the Jordan, with a relatively 'indigenous' view of itself— it thought of its foundation in terms of Jacob, who joined northern Canaan and northern Transjordan in his own story.[26]

3.23 If this rough analysis be allowed, then our finding that northern Transjordan is less problematic for Israel than southern Transjordan implies that the indigenous view of origins (with perhaps expansion *into* Transjordan) is less problematic than the non-indigenous view (entry *from* Transjordan); even if, by a process of mythological assimilation, some of the problems are 'recapitulated' in the Manasseh traditions (§2.34). In the perspective of conquest, Israel must have none of Transjordan, or all. View A, that it must have none, is based ideologically on the demands of cultic purity; but what is the ideological basis for view B, the strong claim to a unified Transjordan? One might speculate that it expresses the interests of the Davidide kings, in their expeditions of conquest into Transjordanian areas which were not traditionally theirs (and which were even under a tabu against Israelite conquest, Moab, etc.; on the importance of Transjordan during the monarchy, cf. Curtis).

3.24 I do not wish to suggest that the indigenous view is 'unideological',[27] but the conquest views show clearer signs of the intentional imposition of ideology. The ideological process of establishing Israel's claim to all Transjordan is complex and illogical. On the one hand, it is assisted by the existence of old 'indigenous' claims to northern Transjordan (especially since the supposed 'tribes' of southern Transjordan tend to sink into obscurity). On the other hand, since Transjordan must be a unity, the conquest of Og's kingdom gets drawn, illogically, into the conquest story. But the sense can by no means be repressed, in the texts, that Israel's presence in northern Transjordan has another basis than conquest. Our findings are consistent with the view that non-indigenous origins were a fiction which Israel had to work hard to maintain.[28]

4.   A test-case: the Jephthah-cycle

4.0   To demonstrate the power of the model I have developed, I shall apply it to a text not previously considered, the Jephthah-cycle in Judg. 10.6–12.7. The model will be found to throw light on numerous exegetical issues in this text.

4.1   Jephthah among the judge-cycles

4.11   This text as it stands is one of the series of judge-cycles considered in Chapter 2 (which compare for the details of the following discussion). It is universally held that these judge-cycles were created for the most part out of older, local stories. Within the section one can easily discern an entirely Transjordanian story about Gilead and the Ammonites, Jephthah and his daughter. Its extent might be 10.17a, 18 (omitting 'the people'), 11.1-3, 5b-11, 30, 31, (32a), 33a, 34-39 (up to 'known a man'); this story would lack a beginning, but 10.8b gives the general idea (and cf. 1 Sam. 11.1a). The acceptance of such a story among those of the other judges implies an acceptance that there are legitimate Transjordanian Israelites; and this story, like the others, has been subsumed to an all-Israel perspective, in particular by the use of standard formulae (10.7; 11.33).

4.12   Only Jephthah of the major judges is Transjordanian, and we must consider whether his cycle has other unique features which may correlate with this. Without doubt, the most striking feature of the framework is that there are *two* national enemies rather than the usual one (10.7), and it is significant for our purposes that one of the two is Cisjordanian (the Philistines) and the other Transjordanian (the Ammonites). But the inclusion of the Philistines is a mystery, since they have absolutely no role to play in the Jephthah account (the initial impression created by 10.7-8 is that the two enemies act together, but it is quickly clear that only the Ammonites are involved). I have in Chapter 2 (2 §§1.24, 1.35) suggested reasons, related to the structure of the books of Judges and 1 Samuel, for the inclusion of the Philistines, and I do not wish to disturb that analysis. But it may be of importance that it is precisely the Transjordanian judge who is unable to deal with the national enemies as a whole (in particular, with a Cisjordanian enemy), so that, however successful such a judgeship may prove to be, there is a level at which it is somehow wrong or irrelevant to the nation's real needs. Such a view would cohere well with the Cisjordanian attitudes towards Transjordan which I have posited.

4.13   The Ammonite oppression has in various ways been put in an 'all Israel' perspective. According to 10.9, the Ammonites *crossed the Jordan* and oppressed the Cisjordanian Israelites (nothing in the rest of the story agrees with this). 10.17-18 labours to make a Gileadite call to arms into a general Israelite muster, and the eventual victory is ascribed to all Israel. But there are other elements of the story which involve both sides of the Jordan, elements having to do with the politics of the Joseph tribes, Ephraim and Manasseh. Jephthah is a 'Gileadite', and, whatever the history of this term may be, it must be taken here to mean 'Transjordanian Manassite' ('Gilead' as a genealogical term, as in 11.1-2, connotes Manasseh, §2.31). According to 12.4 (the text of which is notoriously difficult), the Ephraimites regard the Gileadites as emigrants from the Joseph tribes in Cisjordan. The relationship between Ephraim and Manasseh in this verse is obscure, but it seems likely that rivalry *between* them is part of the scenario. For when the Ephraimites complain of having been left out of the fighting (12.1), Jephthah claims to have invited them (v. 2); however, his recruiting journey in 11.29 included only 'Gilead and Manasseh' (i.e. the two halves of Manasseh?). The potential significance of Jephthah's being a Manassite, a member of the tribe which 'mediates' in living on both sides of the Jordan, is increased by the fact that, within the larger structure of Judges, the previous major judge was a *Cisjordanian* Manassite, Gideon. I shall look at these relationships, from one angle at least, in §4.2.[29]

4.2   The fords of the Jordan

4.21   12.1-6, the incident with the Ephraimites, stands in an obvious transformational relationship to two others, 3.27-29 and 7.24–8.3, and an analysis of the whole set is called for.

4.22   These passages share a general narrative context—the defeat of a Transjordanian enemy (Moab, Midian, Ammon) by Israel under a judge (Ehud, Gideon, Jephthah). They share also two major themes. The first is the occupying of 'the fords of the Jordan', to prevent an enemy from returning to its own territory, and thus to defeat it—a theme found nowhere else in the Bible than in these three passages. The second is calling/not calling the Ephraimites to take a major role in the fighting. Within the 'all Israel' perspective of Judges, Ephraim (the largest tribe) stands, I suggest, for Cisjordanian Israel as a whole (cf. 3.27). This by no means rules out the likelihood that, in the tradition, the whole set of stories had to do with the politics of the Joseph, or rather (to include the Benjaminite Ehud) the Rachel, tribes (§4.13).

4.23   The war against the Transjordanian enemy is a constant within the transformations; there are even intimate links between the three enemies (for Moab and Midian, see §2.224; for Moab and Ammon, §4.342). The other themes are covariable:

3.27-29   Ehud summons Ephraim
at the outset of the campaign
together they hold the fords
thus defeating the whole enemy
no quarrel between Ehud and Ephraim

7.24–8.3   Gideon summons Ephraim
after the decisive battle
Ephraim holds the fords
thus defeating a small part of the enemy
quarrel between Gideon and Ephraim; resolved

12.1-6   Jephthah fails to summon Ephraim
Ephraim arrives after the war is over
irresoluble quarrel between Jephthah and Ephraim
Jephthah holds the fords
thus defeating Ephraim

3.27-29 is unproblematic. 12.1-6 has the same essential elements, but very differently arranged. Jephthah fails to do what Ehud first did, summon Ephraim/Israel to his aid (he claims to have done so [v. 2], but the rest of the story confirms the Ephraimite claim [v. 1] that he did not). Thus the war is over before Jephthah even encounters Ephraim. There is a quarrel, leading to war; Ephraim *becomes* the enemy which Jephthah defeats by holding the fords! Despite the common elements, the distance between the two passages is extreme. But 7.24–8.3 has been organized with great precision to occupy an intermediate place, not only in the sequence, but also in its treatment of the themes. Gideon does summon Ephraim (7.24). But he does not do so immediately; rather, he waits until the war is *partly* over. He and Ephraim act *separately*, and Ephraim finds its part so small that it can even complain (8.1) of not having been summoned at all! There is a quarrel, as in 12.1-6, but one which Gideon can resolve. The three passages could hardly show a clearer progression, in the relationship between the judge and Ephraim, and in the consequences for Israel's unity.

4.24   To unravel the message, we need another variable, and I believe it is to be found in the attachment of the respective judges to Cis- or to Transjordan. Ehud is Cisjordanian, a Benjaminite. Jephthah is equally clearly a Transjordanian. Hence we have the equations

$$\frac{\text{Ehud}}{\text{Jephthah}} = \frac{\text{Cisjordanian}}{\text{Transjordanian}} = \frac{\text{No conflict with Ephraim}}{\text{Total conflict with Ephraim}}$$

Here again, the middle passage perfectly mediates the extremes, for Gideon is a *Cisjordanian* who belongs to Manasseh, the tribe which mediates the two sides of the Jordan.

4.25   We find in all this a double message being conveyed. Judges who become progressively *more Transjordanian* carry out the standard function of the judge, to rid 'all Israel' of foreign enemies. The effect of this is powerfully to *integrate* Cis- and Transjordanian Israelites—representatives of each act for the good of the whole. However, their activities have increasingly bad effects on the unity of 'all Israel', and the 'fords of the Jordan' theme even sets up the equation

$$\frac{\text{Israel}}{\text{Foreign enemies}} = \frac{\text{Transjordanian Israel}}{\text{Cisjordanian Israel}}$$

since the roles of ambusher and ambushed, filled in 3.27-29 and 7.24–8.3 by 'Israel' and 'foreign enemy' are in 12.1-6 filled by 'Gileadites' and 'Ephraimites', that is, Transjordanians and Cisjordanians (it is most instructive to compare this equation with equation b in §1.512). The effect of this is powerfully to divide Cis- from Transjordanian Israelites. My general thesis of a deeply ambiguous view of Transjordan thus receives further confirmation.

4.3　Israel's entitlement to Transjordanian land

4.30　In the main analysis (§2.2), evidence appeared of a deep-seated concern over Israel's entitlement to its Transjordanian holdings; specifically, to the land lying between the Arnon and the Jabbok. One of the passages most relevant to that discussion is precisely in the Jephthah-cycle, namely Judg. 11.12-28, and I omitted it there only in order to preserve the Jephthah-cycle as a test case. It is the Transjordanian judge, but acting (with a clarity unequalled elsewhere in the cycle) as representative of all Israel, who presents Israel's claim to Transjordanian land, and in the most precise legal terms found anywhere. Before proceeding to a direct comparison with the main analysis, it is instructive to consider briefly the context in the Jephthah-cycle.

4.31　In the structure of the Jephthah-cycle, 11.12-28 presents, as it were, a verbal combat preliminary to the military combat; a combat 'won' by Jephthah, after whose lengthy message, in vv. 15-27, the Ammonite king does not care to continue the war of words. Jephthah retells the story of Num. 20–21 and Deut. 2, of Israel's journey from Kadesh to the Jordan. We have here just such a case of enclosing and enclosed narratives as I have dealt with elsewhere (Introduction §5.3); the basic move is to read the two narratives paradigmatically. Here, the enclosed story casts the main story in a definite light. 'Israel' is defined as a negotiator, one who takes the initiative for peaceful solutions. Israel is careful not to preempt a situation by occupying the territory of others—rather it *sends messengers*. Even when it meets with non-response or non-cooperation, Israel avoids conflict (the cases of Edom and Moab). But if, through no fault of Israel's, conflict becomes unavoidable, as in the case of Sihon, then Israel's God teaches the enemy an exemplary lesson. All of this highlights by contrast the moves made by the king of Ammon in the main story. He occupies the disputed territory preemptively. He sends no messengers, but leaves it to Jephthah to do so. And, despite one show of readiness to negotiate (v. 13), which is in fact a naked demand, he fails to answer Jephthah's messengers further (v. 28), thus ranging himself alongside the kings of Edom and Moab, and Sihon, the non-answerers in the enclosed story. Despite his invocation of 'peace' (v. 13) he has really come to 'make war' (v. 27). The topic of the passage being a legal case, the enclosed story hints that one of the litigants is not in good faith from the outset. Ammon's legal claim appears sham before it is even considered on its merits, because Ammon is not a bargainer-in-good-faith, as Israel *is*.[30]

4.32   For the following, the reader will need to refer to my earlier discussion (§§2.21, 2.22), for Jephthah's case raises the same problems, though with new wrinkles. The story he tells is in vv. 16-22, and it corresponds to the account in Num. 20–21, with rather more precision on certain points. Israel, having failed in requests for safe passage to both Edom and Moab (the latter request is not found in Numbers), avoids both. Verse 18 posits with clarity the route undoubtedly intended by Num. 21.10-20. The sequence with Sihon is normal, and the land taken from him is specified in v. 22 exactly as I have suggested in my schematic geography (taking 'the wilderness' to refer to the western border of Ammon; cf. §2.2102).

4.33   The most obvious problem is that Jephthah's history lesson in vv. 16-22 is in no sense a response to the Ammonite king's claim to territory, since Jephthah makes no reference to any (even false) basis for such a claim. What does Jephthah's story have to do with Ammon at all? He does not even mention (as Deut. 2 and, tangentially, Num. 21 do) that Israel *avoided* Ammon. Ammon is simply not part of the story. In the rest of his speech, however, he takes Ammon's claim more seriously. Perceiving, perhaps, that the Ammonite king has accused Israel of relying on 'right of conquest', he invokes the argument from 'divine gift' (vv. 21a, 23-24, 27b; §2.212); but his argument proves vacuous. What he says, essentially, is: 'The territory was specially given to us by Yahweh our god; be content with what your god gives you!' But why should not Ammon's god have given *it* the disputed land, and why should it be Israel's God who decides the matter (v. 27b)? Nor is Jephthah's suggestion of a statute of limitations (v. 26) impressive, for it seems to grant that the Ammonites *had* a real case. All of this suggests that Jephthah is dissatisfied with his case, and that he is disingenuously avoiding reference to the real basis of Ammon's claim.

4.341   In the main analysis, we found evidence of a repressed fear that the land Israel took from Sihon belonged properly to *Moab*, and was therefore no part of the divine gift to Israel. In Judg. 11, we find very much the same situation, except with *Ammon* taking the place of

Moab. But this leads us directly to the most superficially puzzling aspect of Jephthah's whole speech, which is that, while addressing Ammon, he cannot get *Moab* off his mind. His opening statement (v. 15) is that Israel did not take land from Moab or Ammon. For what reason should Moab be even mentioned, let alone *before* Ammon? Next, as every commentator notes, he 'mistakenly' mentions Chemosh the god of Moab, instead of Milcom the god of Ammon, in v. 24. Finally, in v. 25, he says that if Ammon ever had a claim, Moab had at least as good a one—which it never pressed. But why raise the spectre of a Moabite claim at all?

4.342   In the foundation myth of Gen. 19.30-38, Moab and Ammon are the offspring of Lot by his two daughters, and these countries form a pair throughout Israelite tradition.[31] But it is, as I have argued, precisely this myth, along with Gen. 13, which establishes the divine gift of Transjordan to Lot and his offspring. The land in dispute is land which Israel (mythically) 'knows' to be Moabite-Ammonite (§2.223). That it is in the conquest tradition Moab, and in the Judges tradition Ammon, which respectively come to the fore as (real or potential) claimants to the land may have something to do with the contingencies of history and geography. But Moab seems to be accorded a logical priority in a way which goes beyond such contingencies (perhaps as being descended from Lot's *elder* daughter, Gen. 19.37). In the Pentateuch, the centre of Israel's canon, it is Moab's claim which emerges; and when Judges attempts to substitute Ammon's, Moab continues to raise its ugly head even to the extent of a Freudian slip in the divine names! Jephthah comes very close to acknowledging Moab's claim outright (Judg. 11.25), and his argument that Balak never pressed the claim is in some tension with Num. 22–24, and with the Moabite Stone![32]

4.35   Judg. 11.12-28 seems, then, to be a further product of Israel's worry over the proper claim of Lot's descendents to its Transjordanian holdings. The legal (as opposed to mythic) basis for such a claim can only be that the land Israel took from Sihon was land that Sihon had taken from Moab and/or Ammon, and therefore land forbidden to Israel as divinely gifted to an affine; this is expressly said, in regard to Moab, in Num. 21.26. Regardless of the possible existence of a similar basis for a claim by Ammon,[33] the unsuccessful attempt in Judg. 11 to substitute Ammon for Moab may be due to the fact that

Ammon's claim, being less plausible, should be easier to refute. But the unfortunate result of chronicling Jephthah's legal 'victory' is to give further exposure to Israel's shaky legal position![34]

4.4 Transjordanian women; the daughter of Jephthah

4.41 Jephthah is introduced in 11.1-2 as one whose birth is irregular; his mother is a 'foreign woman' (v. 1), or 'another woman' (v. 2), in contrast to the 'wife' (v. 2) who apparently bears 'legitimate' sons. 'Foreign woman' regularly connotes 'prostitute'; but Jephthah can hardly be the son of a common prostitute, since the paternity is known, and, up to his expulsion by his half-brothers, he is a member of his father's household. It is hard to see how his status differs from that of a concubine-son such as Abimelech, so that concubine connection, which we have found to be a feature of the Transjordanian traditions (§2.1) may again be present. Indeed, if Jephthah went, upon his expulsion, to his mother's place (cf. Abimelech again) then she was perhaps another *Aramean* concubine (1 Chron. 7.14 and §2.13), for Tob is in northern Transjordan (Ottosson, 1969: 160)!

4.42 Jephthah's daughter is a Transjordanian woman who dies a virgin. Without wishing either to impugn or to explore the tragic poignancy of her story, it is impossible not to be struck by her formal closeness to our earlier discussion (§§1.533, 2.224). Transjordanian women, we concluded, represent a logical problem in relation to Israelite legitimacy, and the best thing that can happen is for them to move to the west as virgins. It is hard to draw any clear conclusions, but the fact of a Transjordanian line dying out (it is made very clear that Jephthah had no other child), and the special interest in the daughter's virginity, at least make it possible that our previous analysis is relevant. Most interesting of all is the very end of the account (11.40). A female cult developed around Jephthah's daughter, and the text implies that women (virgin daughters?) from *all* Israel annually *went to Transjordan* to celebrate this cult, reversing the 'proper' movement from east to west. I have suggested that, at the deepest level, there is a coding of Cis- and Transjordan as male and female (§3.14). It would be a striking manifestation of this coding if, just as Transjordanian males must fulfil a cultic obligation in the west (§1.521), so must Cisjordanian females in the east! If such an 'explanation' seems extraordinary (and I repeat that we are working at some level entirely different from that of historical custom), is not the text's positing of a Transjordanian female cult equally extra-ordinary?[35]

5.   Appendix: Num. 32, Josh. 22, and a theory of conflict-resolution

5.0   I argued earlier (0.12) for the reading of texts against social-scientific models, as a potential bridge between structuralist and socio-historical approaches; models in particular which are capable of ready application to texts, since texts form most of our data. Purely as an example, and without any claim of its definitive importance, I shall make use in this way of the last chapter of Kenneth E. Boulding's *Confict and Defense*. Our text 'symbolizes' the relations between Cisjordanians and Transjordanians by a double story of conflict and its resolution, and the terms of Boulding's theory seem applicable. To what extent we can read off from such analysis the real attitudes symbolized remains an open question.

5.1   Boulding (308-10) posits three ways in which conflict is brought to an end; avoidance, conquest, and procedural resolution. Avoidance itself takes three forms; one party removing itself from the controverted field, both parties doing so (rare), and one party forcibly removing the other (which at its extreme tends towards 'conquest'). Our stories are obviously cases of procedural resolution, but both avoidance and conquest are raised as possibilities. The controverted field is control over the Transjordanian group, and particularly over its Yahwist practice. The possibility exists of unilateral or even mutual 'avoidance', the Transjordanians setting up a Yahweh-cult in the east (cf. those scholars who hold that the altar in Story II must logically have been in Transjordan, e.g. Ottosson: 134), while the Cisjordanians close the boundary (which is the Transjordanian fear in Story II). Interestingly, Boulding (308) includes among his own examples of avoidance 'A quarrelsome faction within a church splits from it and forms another sect'. But this precisely is not an option; neither can the Cisjordanians tolerate a Yahweh sect, nor can the Transjordanians themselves conceive of their Yahwism as separate. More of an option is conquest, the forcible reintegration of the Yahwist community from the west.

5.2   Again, procedural resolution takes three forms, each with its characteristic means (Boulding: 309-11). They are reconciliation (through processes which, according to Boulding, are inadequately understood), compromise (by bargaining, relatively well understood), and award (by arbitration, with some higher authority, a 'referee'). It is rare to find any of the three in pure form. In Story I, it is compromise which stands out—neither is the issue between Moses and the Transjordanians put to a higher authority, nor is reconciliation particularly stressed. The theory of compromise (Boulding: 313-16) includes the idea of the 'positive-sum game', in which the parties pursue mutual advantage but still try to maximize each its own advantage within the solution reached. This dynamic can be perceived in Story I, as also can another striking feature of compromise theory, 'that the weakest bargainer is frequently in the strongest bargaining position' (315)—Moses, as we have seen, has an uninviting set of options if he declines to compromise. In Story II the situation is different. The upshot seems to be a bargained compromise (cf. 2.23), but the compromise process is obfuscated in the story as it stands. On the one hand, there is a rather overdone reconciliation (Josh. 22.30-31)—reconciliation, as Boulding (311) notes, requires some 'flexibility in the images' which the parties have of each other, but the alteration in the Cisjordanian image of the Transjordanians between vv. 16-20 and 30-31 is too violent. On the other hand, we see a clear element of the *award* situation, in the Transjordanian appeal to Yahweh as higher authority in vv. 22-23.

5.3   Yet there is nothing like an agreement by the parties to submit the case to Yahweh; the Transjordanian appeal to Yahweh's authority is to be read as a reaction to the implicit claim by the Cisjordanians in vv. 16-20 to have Yahweh on their side (cf. 1.6). That Yahweh fails to function as a real referee we may put down to this basic imbalance in the authority situation, due to the fact that it is a Cisjordanian point of view that we are getting. Both stories invoke authority figures, whom one would expect to be neutral vis-à-vis the tribes (Moses, Phinehas), on the Cisjordanian side. A further indication of the Cisjordanian viewpoint is the contrast in the stake which the two sides are presented as having in a solution (cf. Boulding: 312-13, on how much the parties *value* reconciliation)—the Transjordanians indeed have a stake in Yahweh, but what stake do they *really* have in remaining in the east, with all the danger this causes?

5.4   Thus the assessment of the two sides as conflict-producers/

avoiders/enders is rendered more difficult by a bias in the text. Deutsch (6–7) mentions the importance in conflict-theory of the openness of communication, the credibility of mutual perceptions, etc., between the parties. At the level of text-interpretation, we must add the openness of communication and the credibility between narrator and reader! Nonetheless, an assessment may be attempted. Boulding (313) distinguishes between 'the *authoritarian* and the *reconciling* personality' in conflicts. In these terms, it is clear enough that, although the Transjordanians are seen as a *source* of the conflict, it is they also who are the reconcilers, while the Cisjordanians are the authoritarians, the ones who raise the conflict to a high pitch. One's impression in Story I is that Moses' heavy-handed authority covers *anxiety*, even panic, while the Transjordanians have *confidence* in their own powers of compromise. The result of stressing so strongly that legitimate authority lies with the Cisjordanians is that Story I redounds to the credit of the Transjordanians. Is this, perhaps, part of the reason for reopening the matter by means of Story II? Here again, the Cisjordanians are heavy-handed enough, but the narrative succeeds in making the Transjordanians devious, even manipulative, in their management of conflict, to the extent that one may go back and ask whether, even in Story I, they were not merely saying what was necessary to keep the peace, while pursuing their own ends. Is there a message, underlying these accounts of conflict happily resolved, that the hard imposition of authority is the way to deal with those tricky easterners? In connection with the earlier remarks on the recurrence of the conflict (1.42, 1.532), I cannot refrain from a final quote from Boulding (325): 'conflict-producing personalities tend to reproduce themselves in their children'.

NOTES

Notes to Introduction

1. I have argued this at length in Jobling, 1984: 196-97. From reductionism in another sense Lévi-Strauss cannot be exculpated. Cf. Geertz (449): 'The idea... that cultural forms can be treated as texts, as imaginative works built out of social materials, has yet to be systematically exploited. Lévi-Strauss' 'structuralism' might seem to be an exception. But it is only an apparent one, for, rather than taking myths, totem rites, marriage rules, or whatever as texts to interpret, Lévi-Strauss takes them as ciphers to solve, which is very much not the same thing.'

2. For general orientation, cf. Belsey: 103-24; Culler; Eagleton: 127-50. Volume 23 (1982) of *Semeia*, on 'Derrida and Biblical Studies', was in my view a limited success.

3. In the quasi-technical sense in which Barthes (1975) and Kristeva, as well as Greimas (1976) use the word.

Notes to Chapter 1

1. In a famous autobiographical passage, Lévi-Strauss has commented on the importance of Freudian psychoanalysis for the development of his whole structuralist outlook (1973b: 56-59).

2. The reason why I employ the 'generic' term 'man' in this way will become clear from my remarks on feminist exegesis (cf. §3, below). I fully accept the feminist position that the apparent neutrality of generic usage cloaks the patriarchal structuring of the world (e.g. Russell: 93-96, on 'generic nonsense'). My point is that the term *'dm* is used in our text in just this falsely generic way (cf. especially §3.11).

3. The influence of Naidoff (1978) will be clear in this section and elsewhere in my analysis. I agree with his general sense of the text, and appreciate particularly the clarity with which he has perceived the integrity of the agricultural theme. His failure to pursue the significance of the garden seems to me, however, to render his many insights rather haphazard.

4. Casalis (44-45) posits an '"earthly" code', of which 'garden' and 'soil' are the terms. But in 2.15 he reads 'soil' rather than 'garden', on very dubious textual grounds. This skews his whole analysis, so that, though his semantic structures are similar to mine, he does not arrive at a successful narrative segmentation.

5. For the following, cf. White's comment on the absence in our text 'of any unambiguous ... heroes and villains' (1980: 92).

6. ' ... that the sender may be the adversary is very rare. There is only one kind of narrative which can produce this paradoxical formula: the narratives which tell of an extortion' (Barthes, 1974: 31). Barthes is referring to Jacob's wrestling in Gen. 32.23-33 (Eng. 32.22-32), and goes on to speak of the structural 'daring', and of 'the "scandal" represented by the defeat of God'. I do not fully understand his point about 'extortion', but the idea of the defeat, or rather the self-defeat, of God is very much in line with the present analysis. Is it, in the Bible, so 'very rare'?

7. It is noteworthy that my narrative analysis coincides precisely with the 'narrative levels' defined by Patte and Parker (57). Their 'primary level', 2.4b-15 and 3.22-24, defines my model of 'a man to till the earth', while their 'secondary level', 2.16-3.21, is precisely the textual basis for my 'fall' model, which has imposed itself as the dominant one. I suggest that it says something about the 'objectivity' of structural analysis that such diverse approaches should arrive at such compatible results.

8. This opposition of 'dry' and 'wet' is the basis of Casalis's whole analysis, which takes in all the creation and flood material of Genesis, as well as related Mesopotamian literature.

9. For this relationship between sexuality and mortality, cf. *The Epic of Gilgamesh* X (iii) in the Old Babylonian version (Pritchard: 90). Cf. also the comments of Belo (43) on Georges Bataille.

10. The interpretations of Crossan (110) and Kovacs (145-46) are in general agreement with this, but pursue the issues with a greater degree of philosophical generality; the beginning of conceptual differentiation as such is a 'fall'.

11. In different ways, Naidoff (6) and Trible (100-101) have expressed this same point.

12. *Passim* in Jonas, but especially pp. 34-37 for knowledge, and pp. 92-94 for the serpent.

13. For the issues surrounding the two trees, cf. Westermann (252, 288-92). There probably existed an account with only one tree.

14. Naidoff (9) comments on this complexity within Yahweh. Cf. also the remarks of Robertson (29-31) on the 'childlike' and 'adult lessons' conveyed respectively by stories which see God simply and complexly.

15. Cf. Patte and Parker, at the conclusion of their analysis of our text: 'These deep values are *not those upon which the text is focused*' (74-75, their emphasis).

16. The same may be said about the liberation theologies in general, and with the same surprise. For a notable exception, cf. Belo (1981). It is just such an approach as Belo's which feminist exegesis seems to me at present to lack—he, for his part, is not in touch with feminist issues.

Notes to Chapter 2

1. This agrees with the deuteronomic view elsewhere that the 'period of the judges' continues right up to the rise of the monarchy (e.g. 2 Sam. 7.7, 11; 2 Kgs 23.22; and cf. Richter, 1964: 127). In 1 Sam. 12.9-11, Samuel looks back to the period of the judges as *just ended*, and includes himself among the judges.

2. I shall not enter into discussion of what a judge actually was and did (cf. especially Richter, 1964: 127-31; also Boling: 5-9 and other commentaries), including the etymology of *špt̥*, 'to judge', and the fact that the figures we refer to as 'judges' are rarely so called in the text. Some of the issues involved in this debate will arise in the course of my discussion; but in general I mean by 'the judges' the people who led Israel in the period of the judges, doing all the things—judging, teaching, fighting—which are part of leadership (I am quite happy with Richter's conclusion, 1964: 130, that the deuteronomic editors accomplish a composite 'judge-office' from whatever ingredients they received from tradition; that the distinctions were no longer of prime importance to these editors is certainly suggested by the easy sycretism of the judge-office with other offices, particularly in Deborah, Eli, and Samuel).

3. DtrN's positive view of David seems to spoil Veijola's case (120).

4. Part of the 'message', for Buber (83) was that early Israel aimed for an ideal theocracy, but could not maintain it: 'Something has been attempted... but it has failed' (83). This is an important insight (§1.325), and I wish that Buber would say more about why such a message would be relevant to the post-exilic community. A clue is provided by Gottwald (699), in discussing the ongoing importance in Israel of the egalitarianism which, in his view, it developed before the monarchy: 'They (the egalitarian paradigms) were able to produce that extraordinarily self-critical Israelite prophetic movement which aided the survivors of the wreckage of the Israelite states in later times to form various kinds of truncated quasi-tribalized social forms in dispersed communities as well as in a restored Palestinian community.'

5. Polzin (1980) repeatedly (e.g. 162, 167) refers to Judges as anti-ideological, in contrast to the highly ideological beginning to the Deuteronomic History in Joshua. His treatment is always interesting, but it seems to me that he has basically mistaken a clash between opposed ideologies for an avoidance of ideology (if, indeed, the latter is possible).

6. Boling (278) is excellent on the exilic context for the 'debate', whose terms, according to him are 'monarchy', 'tribal confederation', and 'Mosaic ideal'.

7. A debate exists over whether Israel's appeal to Yahweh is to be construed as repentance. The strongest negation comes from Polzin (1980), who insists that Israel's faithlessness to Yahweh continued unbroken through the whole of Judges (e.g. 155-56, 159, 162). Soggin, on the other hand, assumes repentance (4), even to the extent of suggesting that it has

accidentally been omitted from Judg. 2.16 (39). Richter suggests that 2.17 and 2.18-19 represent opposite points of view (1964: 33-34). The unpublished work of Barry Webb (forthcoming as JSOT Supplement 46) has been helpful to me on this as on many other points; he suggests that Israel's appeal may on a given occasion be construed as true repentance or as manipulation (207-208), which is also Samuel's view (1 Sam. 7.3)! It seems to me clear that repentance is integral to the *theory* of the judge-cycles; its absence in practice is an aspect of the break-up of the theory.

8.   Up to v. 19, Israel's faithfulness during the judge's lifetime, and the cyclicality of the scheme, are both less than clear.

9.   No length is given to Shamgar's judgeship, in contrast to the other minor judges. But the 'after' is the trademark of the minor judge, and there is no other way of characterizing him than as a minor judge. On his 'delivering' Israel, cf. note 20.

10.   Note also 13.5: 'he shall *begin* to deliver Israel from the hand of the Philistines'.

11.   The verb is doubtful; LXX quite likely read *pnh*, with the sense of 'repent', rather than the unusual *nhh*, but *lectio difficilior* applies, and in any case we have a reasonable similarity to the 'cry to Yahweh' in the 'normal' cycle.

12.   Veijola (28-29) takes a position related to mine. He too sees Judg. 17–21 as the apostasy which follows the Samson-cycle. But he goes on to interpret 1 Sam. 4 as the foreign oppression resulting from this apostasy, and both elements, apostasy and oppression, as leading into the Samuel-cycle. This fails to take seriously the Eli judge-notice of 4.18, necessitates the exclusion of chs. 1–3 from the cyclical pattern, and fails also, it seems to me, to give due weight to the *persistence* of the Philistine oppression from the time of Jephthah. We are, nonetheless, in agreement on the main point that the judge-cycles continue up to the time of the inauguration of the monarchy. It may be added that Veijola argues for the deuteronomic provenance both of the 'no king in Israel' formula in Judg. 17–21 (16) and of 1 Sam. 7.2-17 as a whole (38).

13.   Even at ch. 12, of course, Samuel does not die. I do not wish to go into this at present, but one obvious point is that he will be needed to anoint David.

14.   Richter has devoted an important article (1965) to this issue. He concludes that the *continuity* of the minor judges is a redactional element, which converges with my position. Of even more interest is his view that the minor-judge notices have developed in some relation to the king-notices of the books of Kings; seen as a system, the minor judges constitute in some respects a proto-monarchy!

15.   We may further note an interest in the *descent* of the judges. The fathers or parents of Gideon, Jephthah, Samson, and Samuel appear significantly. In the latter two cases, of course, the appearance of the parents is in relation to the *call from birth*.

16. It is not clear what we are to make of the reference to Samuel's sons in 12.2, which is at least in tension, if not contradiction, with 8.1-3.

17. Crüsemann (50) holds that kingship was founded in Israel without any expectation of dynastic rule. Whatever the historical likelihood of this my concern is with the assumptions of the text. For a similar instance, cf. note 30.

18. The counter-theme in the Saul tradition, of physical prowess as divine charisma for rulership (9.2; 10.23-24, on which §3.54), is not very clear in Judges. The best parallel is probably Jephthah, sought out by the Gileadites as leader by reason of his prowess (Judg. 11.1, 5-6). But Jephthah is an instance of the *human* choice of a major judge, so that this theme seems theologically at odds with that of lowly origins (cf. also 1 Sam. 16.7!).

19. Cf. Vol. I/3, note 6.

20. Foreign oppression is scarcely a feature of the minor judges. Shamgar (Judg. 3.31) and Tola (10.1) are said to have 'delivered Israel' (a regular *major*-judge formula). Shamgar opposed the Philistines (his similarity to Samson is obvious). It is hard to know how to assess the brief reference to him; but it is striking, at least, that at the first intrusion of the continuous system the later continual oppressor first appears! No foreign oppressor is mentioned in Tola's time; perhaps it was from the internal oppression of Abimelech that he delivered Israel.

21. For the three incidents of holding the fords of the Jordan against an enemy (3.28-29, 7.24-25, and 12.5-6), cf. 3 §4.2.

22. Some commentators see Deut. 17.14-20 as very negative to kingship. This is surely wrong; the passage merely sets stringent limits on kingship. Cf. Veijola: 117.

23. This variety in the material suggests that, methodologically, even subtle divergences from the standard cycle up to Judg. 16 should be considered carefully, whereas thereafter we should concentrate on the *gross* features.

24. Cf. 1 Chron. 17.10 (the parallel 2 Sam. 7.11 should probably be read accordingly); 2 Kgs 23.22 (parallel 2 Chron. 35.18); Isa. 1.26.

25. Buber (59-60, 64-65) sees great importance in this ideal of no human government; cf. especially his reference to 'a commonwealth for which an invisible government is sufficient' (75). He perceives also that the possibility of this ideal is expressed 'by the fact of the pause, for a time, between *shophet* and *shophet*, thus of a *normal* "interregnum"; a fact which was inseparable from the institution of the judgeship . . . ' (83; cf. 76-77, 84).

26. Van Seters (353) agrees with my view of Samuel as 'the last of the victorious judges', and also notes the discrepancy with Samuel's later career (though rather weakly, it seems to me). He is very much in touch with the logic of the text when he goes on to remark, 'The author (Dtr) really regards "the days of Samuel" as closed at the end of chap. 7 but must have a new situation of need to account for the rise of Saul'.

27. 'The scene [i.e. 1 Sam. 8.1-3] has been invented to explain the poeple's demand for a change in the form of government' (Van Seters: 251). Veijola

(55, 68) offers a redaction-critical interpretation: in DtrG, which is positive
to monarchy, 8.1-5 is a natural transition from judgeship to monarchy, while
8.6ff. belongs to DtrN, and stands in contradiction to what precedes. Buber
(76) is closest to my view; he refers to 'the delinquency of Samuel himself in
relation to the anti-dynastic temper of the judgeship (I Samuel 8.1-5), a
delinquency not yet sufficiently recognized in its significance for the
Samuelic crisis'. But even this does not do justice, at a literary level, either to
the abruptness or to the necessity of the logical break which this brief
passage achieves. I hope that this essay is sufficient recognition of Samuel's
delinquency!

28. This point can perhaps be more firmly established by reference to the
'gaps', Judg. 8.33–9.57 and chs. 17–21. Whereas in the standard cycle
Israel's fault is to go after *foreign* gods (2.12, with which cf. particularly
10.6), with the consequence of *foreign* oppression, in these two sections the
apostasy is, as it were, *internal*, and the consequence is the extreme of
internecine strife, the *internal* oppression of Israelite by Israelite. (For cultic
offence in Judg. 17–21, cf. §1.1212; in chs. 8–9, it is Gideon's false Yahweh-
worship, 8.27, which leads to Abimelech's oppression, with which cf. Gros
Louis's reference to Abimelech as Israel's 'internal enemy' [155]). The
theological point can as well be expressed through the code of Israel's
internal situation as through that of its external relations.

29. In chs. 13–15, Saul is always on the wrong side of cultic issues; indeed
it is these cultic offences which bring about his fall (Jobling, 1976). The
claims made on his behalf as a deliverer (§1.243) will by no means be borne
out in his later career; the defeat of the Ammonites will be his only lasting
success, and it will be left to David (founder of a permanent kingship) to
defeat the Philistines and the 'enemies round about'. As to dynasty, I have
argued elsewhere that it is precisely the non-continuance of the dynasty of
Saul which is the next theological problem that the Deuteronomic History
has to solve, and that this problem dominates the whole of 1 Sam. 13–31 (see
Vol. I/1); as soon as 13.13-14 we learn that Saul's kingship *was to have been*
hereditary.

30. Crüsemann (48ff.) argues that Gideon's making of an ephod is wholly
compatible with his refusal of the kingship, since the ephod belongs precisely
to Israel's pre-monarchical faith. In relation to the tradition behind the text,
this possibility is interesting. But the present text uncompromisingly sees
Gideon's action as apostasy. Buber (73) is likewise unable to accept any
ambiguity in Gideon, after his epoch-making declaration in v. 23, and
blames the people: ' . . . the ephod which Gideon erected as sanctuary of his
Lord and which the people made into the centre of a Baal cult'.

31. For Richter's point (1964: 109) that 8.33-35 serves to shift the blame
for the aftermath from Abimelech to Israel, cf. §2.242.

32. Polzin (1980: 173) sees it as a sign of this negativity that the name
Yahweh is never used in ch. 9.

33. On the technicalities, cf. for example Boling (162-63). The absence of comment in scholarly literature on my 'obvious' etymology is quite remarkable. Perhaps it bespeaks a fear that the text might seem 'fictional' if we admitted such means of expressing meaning (was the narrator at liberty to choose names?). Buber (73-74) allows the pun, but argues that Abimelech gave the name to himself!

34. Fritz (132), following Veijola (106-107), assumes the Jotham material to have been added redactionally 'to fill out the story into a basic debate over Abimelech's kingship'. This, certainly, is the effect of the material.

35. Other scholars (e.g. Lindars, Fritz: 140, Boling: 174) take the view that the fable is not anti-monarchical in principle; but the only coherent interpretation from this perspective known to me is that of Lindars (365-66), who sees in it polemic against those who are worthy of kingship, but who refuse it for selfish reasons, thus assuring that it will go to the unworthy. But this interpretation does not cohere well with v. 15a (§2.323), and Lindars, in fact, holds that an original ending to the fable, now lost, had the bramble accepting the kingship (362).

36. It is well established that 'take refuge in the shade of' is a standard metaphor for a king's function of protecting his people (Crüsemann: 21; cf. Lam. 4.20). The bramble's joke is all the better in that it works at two levels.

37. Many scholars, of course, deny that v. 15b belongs to the original fable (e.g. Crüsemann: 19).

38. Crüsemann (22-27) offers an excellent cross-cultural examination of this type of fable.

39. Fritz (133), following Veijola (110-11), sees vv. 16b-19a as a separate section belonging to a very late redactional stage.

40. The scene in 9.1-6, and to some extent its context, has an intricate set of parallels in 2 Kgs 8.16–14.16 (cf. Liverani)—the slaying of seventy sons of a king (10.7); the hiding of a king's son (whose name happens to be Joash, 11.1-3); the theme of usurpation; even the fable in 14.9. I do not, in this essay, delve into the possibilities for 'intertextual' analysis, but I do draw upon a few features of the 2 Kings material when they seem suggestive for my analysis of Judges.

41. 'The slaughter of the seventy, like the decapitation of Ahab's seventy sons in II Kings 10.1-11, clearly marks the end of an era or dynasty and the beginning of the new regime' (Boling: 171; cf. Crüsemann: 39). But we do not, in Judg. 9, have the end of a dynasty; Abimelech is, after all, Gideon's son. Perhaps the 2 Kings reference is, though, a marker of the great distance (in worthiness, etc.) between Gideon and Abimelech. Another text which might be drawn into the discussion is 2 Sam. 13.23-36.

42. 'Gideon did become a dynast, in fact if not in name' (Webb: 221). Soggin sees in the family data of 8.30-31 an indication of 'the regal character of Gideon' (159).

43. It is also tempting to compare Jotham's ironic view of the mutuality of

Abimelech and his people (vv. 19-20) with Samuel's 'you and your king' (1 Sam. 12.15, 25).

Notes to Chapter 3

1. Most of this chapter has appeared in a slightly different form (Jobling, 1980a). In the earlier version I included (198-99) a reading of Num. 32 and Josh. 22 in relation to a recent theory of conflict. I have included this below as an appendix (§5).

2. 4.12-13 would need to be studied as part of the whole account of the Crossing of the Jordan, which is beyond the scope of the present analysis.

3. This point is somewhat obscured by the odd reference to Manasseh in Josh. 22.7a, on which cf. note 21.

4. The version in Deut. 1.20-46 differs considerably. In this case, though, one has narrative justification for neglecting Deuteronomy, since Moses cannot 'recall' it in Numbers!

5. The presence of Joshua as an actor in Story I may, however, make the reference to him here important at some other level.

6. There is, of course, no scholarly agreement about the location of the altar (e.g. Ottosson, 1984: 102). But most of the discussion is about a hypothetical historical altar, not the textual one. Coats (188) refreshingly takes the text at face value, and tries to work out what it intends.

7. No doubt the textual stratagem which I am suggesting was assisted by the fact that namings customarily come at the end of aetiological stories. But the case is quite different here. In an aetiological story, the name depends on some feature of the story. Here, the story depends on the name; or rather, there would be no story if the name were not withheld!

8. The narrator, indeed, seems to have caught this secretiveness, in withholding until v. 28 the information, presumably vital, that the altar was a copy of the one in Yahweh's tabernacle!

9. This summary of the preceding discussion can be plotted on the *semiotic square* (cf. Aristotle's logical square, discussed by Güttgemanns: 64-68):

On each side, the upper state implies the lower, but not *vice versa* (i.e. integrity can exist only if there is no division, but there can be a state of non-division even in the absence of integrity, etc.). The upper two states are contraries—the cannot both obtain simultaneously; the lower two are subcontraries—they cannot both *not* obtain simultaneously. All this lies in the theory of the square itself, not in our particular case. To interpret: The Cisjordanians are in the 'either/or' situation of the top line; if not integrity, then division. They read the vertical implications upwards as well as downwards, which simple means that they *equate* integrity with non-division, etc. (making integrity and division into contradictories instead of contraries). The Transjordanians are in the 'both/and' situation of the bottom line, insisting upon *both* non-integrity *and* non-division. According to the theory of Greimas (1970: 175-78), narrative movement follows the sequence top left, bottom right, top right, bottom left, and finally back to top left. Story II follows the proper movement; it begins with the integrity of Cisjordanians and Transjordanians (before the parting), and moves to non-integrity (the parting), division (the quarrel), and non-division (the resolution of the quarrel). The final move, back to integrity, does not occur; but it is implied in the obligation which the Transjordanians take upon themselves, to return to the west for the cultic service of Yahweh.

10. It seems that two accounts have been awkwardly juxtaposed in Num. 25 (vv. 1-5 and vv. 6-18) but both have the element of seduction by women.

11. That the narrative is working hard to achieve this result is clear from the fact that all the allusions are in the 'angry' speeches, which I have shown, both in Story I and in Story II, to be narratively awkward (§§1.113, 1.22).

12. Ottosson, following Mowinckel, speculates that Num. 32 and Josh. 22 are together the result of theologizing in the priestly schools, which were concerned for 'the harmony of the 12 tribe amphictyony, although the River Jordan was to cut off the Transjordan tribes from those on the western bank' (1969: 74-75). There may, then, be historical support for my purely literary suggestions.

13. The cases in Num. 2; 7; 10, where Judah leads, are not really lists. From lists of Cisjordanian tribes, Reuben is of course absent; and in a case like Josh. 21 his apparent demotion is accountable by geography.

14. See 1 Chron. 5.1-2. It is odd that, although this passage claims that the precedence passed to Joseph, it is actually Judah which appears first in these genealogies.

15. This genealogy is ostensibly of *Cisjordanian* Manasseh (for the Transjordanian half, cf. 5.23-26), but the 'Aramean' confirms Machir's Transjordanian connection. The whole genealogy of is in poor shape; 'Asriel' seems to be a mistake based on Num. 26.31, etc., and the tradition is out of kilter with Gen. 50.23.

16. The most frequent departure from the norm is the attachment of the east Jordan valley north of Jabbok to the holding south of Jabbok, both as Sihon's (Josh. 12.3) and as Gad's (Josh. 13.26-27; cf. Deut. 3.17); even this preserves the first part of the equation. For the details, Ottosson, 1969: 78, 109-10, 114, 119.

17. See §2.2102. Ammon is something of a problem in both versions; the avoidance of it is not mentioned in Numbers, where it would make sense (since Israel's route takes it close to Ammon's border), while it is mentioned in Deuteronomy, where it makes less sense (since the direct route through Moab need not take Israel close to Ammon's border). This all hints at a deeper significance for Ammon than either of these texts suggests. My later analysis of Judg. 11.12-28 will help unravel the matter (§4.3).

18. So Coats (184), in line with his general case that the Numbers sequence belongs to the Wilderness, and not yet to the Conquest, theme, in the structure of Israel's traditions. Hulst (186) claims that the relevant texts make Moses, not Yahweh, the 'giver' of Transjordan; but Coats (189-90) sees even Moses' involvement as carefully played down. On 'divine gift' in the Deuteronomist, see Ottosson (1969: 98-101). On the 'parallel' defeat of Og, cf. §2.241.

19. Names such as 'The Plains of Moab' do not necessarily imply, of course, territory currently held by Moab—the name could enshrine previous political realities. But, as the next paragraph will show, the problem of legitimacy applies to Israel's holding of land which *ever has been Moabite*.

20. Ottosson pays attention to the Genesis texts (1969: 52, 57, 241; 1984: 99). But he does not allow much force to the prior claim of Lot's descendants. This is mainly because he sees Lot to have *lost* his inheritance in connection with the events of Gen. 14. His reasoning here is mysterious to me. A more (but still not very) plausible case might be made that Lot's offspring lost the inheritance because of the incest of Gen. 19.30-38; this disgrace will at any rate have lain behind (provided 'permission' for) the mythic revision.

21. Along these lines, an interpretation of the odd interpolation of Josh. 22.7a may be suggested; it stands as a marker of the fact that it is a single entity, 'brethren', which is separating. Historically, there was a close attachment of Transjordan to the northern tribes; cf. Ottosson, 1969: 14, 73, and also E. Nielsen's suggestion in Hulst (172) that Judah, but not northern Israel, regarded the Jordan as a boundary.

22. I find myself in a large measure of agreement with Coats, in his view that the 'conquest' elements in Numbers are fragmentary, poorly integrated, and lacking in features belonging to the authentic Conquest theme of Joshua. In line with his thesis, he stresses (much more firmly than my other main secondary source, Ottosson, cf. note 28) how strong was the consciousness of the Jordan as a boundary (e.g. 188-89). But in my method anomalies are pointers to meaning, and it seems to me that Coats fails to take the conquest elements in Numbers seriously enough precisely in their anomalousness. For example, the north of Jabbok references, fragmentary as they are (Num. 21.33-35; 32.39-42), have the proper conquest features, and must surely point to something important.

23. Verse 5 makes the arithmetic precise; the inheritances of the five

daughters, joined to those of their five 'great uncles', make up a total of ten portions for Cisjordanian Manasseh. This over against Gilead and Bashan (two units) for the Transjordanian moiety. It is tempting to see, in this ten and two pattern, the division of all Israel into tribes roughly recapitulated in the division of Manasseh into portions (§§2.242, 2.34)!

24. Cf. §4.2, on Judg. 12.1-6. Of great importance also is Ottosson's parallel between Rachel and Jephthah's daughter under the category of settlement of land disputes (1969: 48).

25. As examples of its explanatory potential, the *fighting styles* of the two sides, authoritarian (Cisjordanians) and conciliatory/manipulative (Transjordanians), on which cf. §5.4, can be looked at in terms of male-female stereotypes, while the whole issue of *precedence* takes on new dimensions.

26. This is all fairly standard, and in line with Gottwald's own views. A fuller analysis would require consideration of all the Aramean connections of Israel's ancestors, including the apparent connubium (Isaac-Rebekah, Jacob and his wives).

27. The great importance of the Jacob traditions for the Bible's ideological view of Transjordan was brought home to me by Ottosson (1969: 36-52) after the outlines of my analysis were established, and I have paid little attention to these traditions (but cf. note 35). But one matter is important enough to require comment. Ottosson (51) claims that, in his fight at Penuel on the Jabbok (Gen. 32.22-32), 'Jacob won the right to Transjordan', by which he means the larger Transjordan of the conquest traditions. That the Penuel myth embodies a claim to Transjordanian land south of Jabbok is contrary to the case I am arguing. This land was given to Moab and Ammon in the Abraham-Lot stories of Gen. 13 and 19; Ottosson refers to this, but I am not clear whether he sees the Jacob-Esau mythology as in conflict with that of Abraham and Lot, or whether he has in mind his argument elsewhere that Lot's inheritance was forfeited (note 20). In any case, it seems to me that, in the present biblical sequence, a single consistent mythology has been created. Moab and Ammon having received their inheritance, which extends north to the Jabbok, Jacob and Esau may receive such eastern territory as lies north and south of Moab-Ammon. Whatever the origin of the Penuel myth, it seems now, so far as ideological geography is concerned, simply to provide a connection between Jacob and the Jabbok, and hence to give Jacob's authority to the Jabbok as a frontier (this is my 'C' view of Israel's land in §3.22). This reading fits in with the fact that Jacob, after the Penuel meeting, does not travel further south in Transjordan to affirm his ownership, but goes directly to Cisjordan.

28. Cf. Ottosson (1984: 100): 'The Deuteronomist's way of working with textual structures . . . demands with all desirable clarity a negative evaluation of the "Conquest" understood as a tangible historical event datable to 1200 or even earlier.' I have drawn largely on Ottosson's work, not least because

he clearly sees the biblical texts as expressions of ideology (e.g. 1969: 9-14). But he often seems content to accept the text's point of view, even when the ideological stresses are plainest. For example, he shrugs off the 'accidental' quality of Israel's conquest of Transjordan (1969: 135), and above all the 'prior claim' of Moab and Ammon (161-69, where he accepts Jephthah's arguments in Judg. 11.12-28; cf. §4.3). The harder the text must work to establish ideology, the more the ideology is to be questioned; this is why a 'deconstructive' approach (Introduction §4) seems to me to be called for.

29. An inviting line which I shall not pursue here (but cf. §4.41) is the obvious parallels between Gideon's son Abimelech and Jephthah (irregular parentage, association with 'worthless fellows', etc.).

30. The parallel between enclosed and enclosing stories is made unmistakably clear by a number of stylistic elements, for example 'sending messengers' (vv. 12, 14, 17, 19), 'not listening' (vv. 17, 28, cf. 20), and 'possessing/dispossessing' (vv. 21-24).

31. E.g. 'sons of Lot' (Deut. 2.9, 19), and the compounding of Chemosh and Molech in 1 Kgs 11.7. A great many passages could be adduced.

32. For recent evidence that Balaam, the counsellor of the King of Moab in Num. 22–24, was an Ammonite, cf. Ottosson, 1984: 103.

33. Josh. 13.25 indicates that Gad took some Ammonite territory (Ottosson's assumption, 1969: 126-27, that this refers, not to land originally Ammonite, but to land taken by Ammon in circumstances like those of Judg. 11, begs the question). Jer. 49.1, conversely, speaks of the Ammonites' dispossessing Gad. In the light of this, is it possible to hazard the suggestion that a further rationalization is in play, namely that Reuben took formerly Moabite, and Gad formerly Ammonite, land from Sihon? This is first of all simply a logical suggestion—the two pairs, Reuben-Gad and Moab-Ammon, are givens, and will tend to be mapped onto each other in some way. But it may be added that the land which Israel takes in Num. 21.21-32 is oddly 'doubled' in v. 32; a second lot of land, around Jazer, is taken—and v. 24 has associated just this second lot of land with the Ammonites!

34. The reader will perceive the need, at this point, for some consideration of the opposition north *vs.* south of the Jabbok. The text of Judges does not seem to provide sufficient data for analysis, but a few comments may be made. Though Jephthah is a Manassite, the main action of his story takes place *south* of the Jabbok (according to the usual location of Mizpah, but also because no possible sense could be made of an Ammonite claim to land north of the Jabbok). Northern Transjordan appears only as the place of Jephthah's retreat after his expulsion from his father's house (11.3), and as part of the extent of his recruiting drive (v. 29). For a Manassite to be living south of the Jabbok does not agree with the land-allotment traditions. But what the account achieves is a unifying of Transjordan under the flag, as it were, of Manasseh; the less disputed legitimacy of the north is implicitly claimed for the south by having a Manassite argue the case for legitimacy!

35. Ottosson (1969: 48-50, 158-59) rightly makes much of the parallels between Jephthah's daughter and Rachel in Gen. 31. Both are involved in disputes over land ownership (cf. §2.3) at Mizpah of Gilead, and each is the object of a death sentence unwittingly pronounced. He explores the possible connections of both with fertility rites (involving ritual weeping), and notes that Jephthah's mother's being a 'foreign woman' may be a further hint in the same direction.

WORKS CONSULTED

Barthes, R.
1975   *S/Z*. Trans. R. Miller. London: Jonathan Cape.
Barthes, R. and others
1974   *Structural Analysis and Biblical Exegesis*. Trans. A.M. Johnson, Jr. Pittsburgh: Pickwick Press.
Belo, F.
1981   *A Materialist Reading of the Gospel of Mark*. Trans. Matthew J. O'Connell. Maryknoll: Orbis Books.
Belsey, C.
1980   *Critical Practice*. London and New York: Methuen.
Boling, R.G.
1975   *Judges: Introduction, Translation, and Commentary*. Garden City: Doubleday.
Borges, J.L.
1970   *Labyrinths: Selected Stories & Other Writings*. Ed. Donald A. Yates and James E. Irby. London: Penguin.
Boulding, Kenneth E.
1962   *Conflict and Defense*. New York: Harper & Row.
Buber, M.
1967   *The Kingdom of God*. Trans. Richard Scheimann. New York: Harper & Row.
Carroll, M.P.
1977   'Leach, Genesis, and Structural Analysis: A Critical Evaluation'. *American Ethnologist* 4: 671-77.
Casalis, M.
1976   'The Dry and the Wet: A Semiological Analysis of Creation and Flood Myths'. *Semiotica* 17: 35-67.
Coats, G.W.
1976   'Conquest Traditions in the Wilderness Theme'. *JBL* 95: 177-90.
Crossan, J.D.
1980   'Response to White: Felix Culpa and Foenix Culprit'. *Semeia* 18: 107-11.
Crüsemann, F.
1978   *Der Widerstand gegen das Königtum: Die antiköniglichen Texte des Alten Testamentes und der Kampf um den frühen israelitischen Staat*. Neukirchen: Neukirchener Verlag.
Culler, J.
1982   *On Deconstruction: Theory and Criticism after Structuralism*. Ithaca and London: Cornell University Press.
Culley, R.C.
1980   'Action Sequences in Genesis 2–3'. *Semeia* 18: 25-33.
Curtis, J.B.
1961   '"East is East . . . "'. *JBL* 80: 355-63.
De George, R.T. and F.M., eds.
1972   *The Structuralists from Marx to Lévi-Strauss*. Garden City: Doubleday.
Deutsch, Morton
1973   *The Resolution of Conflict*. New Haven: Yale University Press.

Eagleton, T.
1983   *Literary Theory: An Introduction*. Oxford: Basil Blackwell.
Ellis, P.F.
1963   *The Men and the Message of the Old Testament*. Collegeville: The Liturgical Press.
Fetterley, J.
1978   *The Resisting Reader: A Feminist Approach to American Fiction*. Bloomington: Indiana University Press.
Fiorenza, E.S.
1983   *In Memory of Her: A Feminist Theological Reconstruction of Christian Origins*. New York: Crossroad.
1984   *Bread Not Stone: The Challenge of Feminist Biblical Interpretation*. Boston: Beacon Press.
Freedman, D.N.
1976   'Deuteronomic History, The'. *IDBS*: 226-28.
Fritz, V.
1982   'Abimelech und Sichem in Jdc. IX'. *VT* 32: 129-44.
Geertz, C.
1973   *The Interpretation of Cultures*. New York: Basic Books.
Gottwald, N.K.
1979   *The Tribes of Yahweh: A Sociology of the Religion of Liberated Israel, 1250-1050 B.C.E.*. Maryknoll: Orbis Books.
Greimas, A.J.
1966   *Sémantique structurale: Recherche de méthode*. Paris: Larousse.
1970   *Du sens: Essais sémiotiques*. Paris: éditions du Seuil.
1976   *Maupassant*. Paris: éditions du Seuil.
Greimas, A.J. and Courtes, J.
1983   *Semiotics and Language: An Analytical Dictionary*. Bloomington: Indiana University Press.
Gros Louis, K.R.R.
1974   'The Book of Judges'. K.R.R. Gros Louis and others, eds., *Literary Interpretations of Biblical Narratives*: 141-62. Nashville: Abingdon Press.
Güttgemanns, E.
1976   'Generative Poetics'. *Semeia* 6: 1-220.
Hulst, A.R.
1965   'Der Jordan in den alttestamentlichen Überlieferungen'. *Oudtestamentische Studiën* 14: 162-88.
Jensen, H.J.L.
1982   'A Structural Analysis of Some Old Testament Narratives'. Unpublished Ph.D. dissertation (Danish), University of Aarhus.
Jobling, D.
1976   'Saul's Fall and Jonathan's Rise: Tradition and Redaction in 1 Samuel 14.1-46'. *JBL* 95: 367-76.
1978   *The Sense of Biblical Narrative: Three Structural Analyses in the Old Testament*. Sheffield: JSOT. (Repr. 1986 as *The Sense of Biblical Narrative: Structural Analyses in the Hebrew Bible*, Volume I).
1979   'Structuralism, Hermeneutics, and Exegesis: Three Recent Contributions to the Debate'. *Union Seminary Quarterly Review* 34: 135-47.
1980a   'The Jordan a Boundary: A Reading of Numbers 32 and Joshua 22'. P.J. Achtemeier, ed., *Society of Biblical Literature Seminar Papers*: 183-207. Chico: Scholars Press.

1980b   'The Myth Semantics of Genesis 2.4b–3.24'. *Semeia* 18: 41-49.
1983   'Judges 11.12-28: Constructive and Deconstructive Analysis'. J.N. Deely
         and M.D. Lenhart, eds., *Semiotics 1981*: 521-28. New York and London:
         Plenum Press.
1984   'Lévi-Strauss and the Structural Analysis of the Hebrew Bible'. R.L.
         Moore and F.E. Reynolds, eds., *Anthropology and the Study of Religion*:
         192-211. Chicago: Center for the Scientific Study of Religion.

Jonas, H.
1958   *The Gnostic Religion*. Boston: Beacon Press.

Kovacs, B.W.
1980   'Structure and Narrative Rhetoric in Genesis 2–3: Reflections on the
         Problem of Non-Convergent Structuralist Exegetical Methodologies'.
         Semeia 18: 139-47.

Kristéva, J.
1968   'La productivité dite texte'. *Communications* 11: 59-83.

Lane, M., ed.
1970   *Introduction to Structuralism*. New York: Basic Books.

Leach, E.
1961   'Lévi-Strauss in the Garden of Eden'. *Transactions of the New York
         Academy of Sciences* 23: 386-96.
1969   *Genesis as Myth and Other Essays*. London: Jonathan Cape.

Lemaire, A.
1982   'Galaad et Makir: Remarques sur la tribu de Manassé à l'est du Jourdain'.
         VT 31: 39-61.

Lévi-Strauss, C.
1963a   'Réponse à quelques questions'. *Esprit* 31: 628-53.
1963b   *Structural Anthropology*. Trans. C. Jacobson and B.G. Schoepf. New
         York: Basic Books.
1970   *The Raw and the Cooked*. Trans. J. and D. Weightman. London: Jonathan
         Cape.
1973a   *From Honey to Ashes*. Trans. J. and D. Weightman. London: Jonathan
         Cape.
1973b   *Tristes Tropiques*. Trans. J. and D. Weightman. London: Jonathan Cape.
1978   *The Origin of Table Manners*. Trans. J. and D. Weightman. London:
         Jonathan Cape.
1981   *The Naked Man*. Trans. J. and D. Weightman. London: Jonathan Cape.

Lindars, B.
1973   'Jotham's Fable: A New Form-Critical Analysis'. *Journal of Theological
         Studies* 24: 55-66.

Liverani, M.
1974   'L'histoire de Joas'. *VT* 24: 438-53.

Malamat, A.
1973   'Tribal Societies: Biblical Genealogies and African Lineage Systems'.
         Archives européennes de sociologie 14: 126-36.

McCarthy, D.J.
1965   'II Samuel 7 and the Structure of the Deuteronomic History'. *JBL*
         84:131-38.
1973   'The Inauguration of Monarchy in Israel: A Form-Critical Study of I
         Samuel 8–12'. *Interpretation* 27: 401-12.

Miller, J.M. and G.M. Tucker
1974   *The Book of Joshua*. Cambridge: Cambridge University Press.

Moore, G.F.
1895   *A Critical and Exegetical Commentary on Judges*. Edinburgh: T. & T. Clark.

Naidoff, B.D.
1978   'A Man to Work the Soil: A New Interpretation of Genesis 2–3'. *JSOT* 5: 2-14.

Noth, M.
1981   *The Deuteronomistic History*. Sheffield: JSOT.

Ottosson, M.
1969   *Gilead*. Trans. J. Gray. Lund: Gleerup.
1984   'Tradition and History, with Emphasis on the Composition of the Book of Joshua'. K. Jeppesen and B. Otzen, eds., *The Productions of Time: Tradition History and Old Testament Scholarship*: 81-106. Sheffield: Almond Press.

Patte, D.
1976   *What is Structural Exegesis?*. Philadelphia: Fortress Press.

Patte, D. and J.F. Parker
1980   'A Structural Exegesis of Genesis 2–3'. *Semeia* 18: 55-75.

Polzin, R.M.
1977   *Biblical Structuralism: Method and Subjectivity in the Study of Ancient Texts*. Philadelphia: Fortress Press.
1980   *Moses and the Deuteronomist: A Literary Study of the Deuteronomic History*. New York: Seabury Press.

Pritchard, J.B., ed.
1969   *Ancient Near Eastern Texts Relating to the Old Testament*. 3rd edition. Princeton: Princeton University Press.

Propp, V.
1968   *Morphology of the Folktale*. Trans. L. Scott. 2nd edition by L.A. Wagner. Austin: University of Texas Press.

Richter, W.
1964   *Die Bearbeitung des 'Retterbuches' in der deuteronomischen Epoche*. Bonn: Hanstein.
1965   'Zu den "Richtern Israels"'. *Zeitschrift für die alttestamentliche Wissenschaft* 77: 40-72.
1966   *Traditionsgeschichtliche Untersuchungen zum Richterbuch*. Bonn: Hanstein.

Robertson, D.
1977   *The Old Testament and the Literary Critic*. Philadelphia: Fortress Press.

Russ, J.
1975   *The Female Man*. New York: Bantam.

Russell, L.
1974   *Human Liberation in a Feminist Perspective*. Philadelphia: Westminster Press.

Ryan, M.
1982   *Marxism and Deconstruction: A Critical Articulation*. Baltimore and London: Johns Hopkins University Press.

Seebass, H.
1981   'Machir im Ostjordanland'. *VT* 32: 496-503.

Showalter, E.
1983   'Critical Cross-Dressing: Male Feminists and the Woman of the Year'. *Raritan* 3: 130-49.

Soggin, A.
    1972   *Joshua*. Trans. R.A. Wilson. London: SCM Press.
Sumner, W.A.
    1968   'Israel's Encounters with Edom, Moab, Ammon, Sihon, and Og according
            to the Deuteronomist'. *VT* 18: 216-28.
Trible, P.
    1978   *God and the Rhetoric of Sexuality*. Philadelphia: Fortress Press.
Van Seters, J.
    1983   *In Search of History: Historiography in the Ancient World and the Origins
            of Biblical History*. New Haven and London: Yale University Press.
Veijola, T.
    1977   *Das Königtum in der Beurteilung der deuteronomistischen Historiographie:
            Eine redaktionsgeschichtliche Untersuchung*. Helsinki: Academia Scientiarum
            Fennica.
Webb, B.G.
    1985   'Theme in the Book of Judges: A Literary Study of the Book in its
            Finished Form'. Unpublished Ph.D. dissertation, University of Sheffield.
            Volume I. [Forcoming in JSOT Supplement Series]
Wellhausen, J.
    1963   *Die Composition des Hexateuchs und der historischen Bücher des alten
            Testaments*. Berlin: Walter de Gruyter.
Westermann, C.
    1984   *Genesis 1–11: A Commentary*. Trans. J.J. Scullion. London: SPCK.
White, H.C.
    1979   'Structural Analysis of the Old Testament Narrative'. M.J. Buss, ed.,
            Encounter with the Text: Form and History in the Hebrew Bible: 45-66.
            Philadelphia: Fortress Press.
    1980   'Direct and Third Person Discourse in the Narative of the "Fall"'. *Semeia*
            18: 91-106.

Abbreviations of Journals, etc.

IDBS   *The Interpreter's Dictionary of the Bible*, Supplementary Volume
JBL   *Journal of Biblical Literature*
VT   *Vetus Testamentum*

An earlier version of Chapter 1 appeared in *Semeia*, published by Scholars Press, and
earlier versions of parts of Chapter 3 appeared in publications by Plenum Press and
the Center for the Scientific Study of Religion (cf. above, 'Works Consulted', Jobling,
1980b, 1983, 1984). The material is re-used here by the permission of these publishers.

INDEX OF AUTHORS

JOURNAL FOR THE STUDY OF THE OLD TESTAMENT

Supplement Series